THE AMERICAN FAMILY COOKBOOK

CHARTWELL BOOKS, INC.

THE AMERICAN FAMILY COOKBOOK

PAMELA WESTLAND

Published in the United States by
Chartwell Books Inc.
A division of Book Sales Inc,
110, Enterprise Avenue,
Secaucus,
New Jersey,
07094

Produced by Winchmore Publishing
Services Ltd,
40 Triton Square,
London W1.

Printed in Yugoslavia

CONTENTS

INTRODUCTION

Think of American home cooking and you think of what? A coming-together of some of the finest ingredients in the world and stimulating variety of cultures; of the regional differences and strong local traditions. Of a whole new world of cooking, in fact.

Trace the fortunes of the early Pilgrims, their struggle to adapt their own cooking traditions to a new crop of ingredients, and their rejoicing, in the first Thanksgiving dinner, when they succeeded.

Discover the subtle delights of Creole cooking which flourished from the twin influences of France and Spain on the Southern States, and the anything-but-subtle effect the Mexican origins have had on the Tex-Mex cuisine of the South-West.

Marvel at the imaginative "soul food" dishes that came from Africa with the cotton slaves, tasty meals composed of beans and rice and next to nothing besides, and the diligence of the cowboy cooks, forever on the move, who produced man-sized meals with fresh daily bread.

Turn back the clock with some real old-fashioned baking; entertain American barbecue-style with steamed clams or shrimp gumbo, or learn how varied, delicious and even healthy fast-food snacks can be.

In short, sample with us a taste of American family cooking.

GLOSSARY OF TERMS

American and British readers might find it helpful to know what various ingredients are called on the other side of the Atlantic.

British	American
apple purée	apple sauce
aubergine	egg plant
back bacon	Canadian bacon
bacon rashers	bacon slices
belly of pork	fresh picnic shoulder
bicarbonate of soda	baking soda
biscuits	cookies
black olives	ripe olives
broad beans	fava beans
cake icing	frosting
caster sugar	superfine sugar
cheese biscuits	crackers
chicory	endive
cooking chocolate	unsweetened cooking chocolate
cornflour	corn starch
courgette	zucchini
demerara sugar	light brown sugar
desiccated coconut	shredded coconut
digestive biscuits	graham crackers
double cream	whipping cream
essence	extract
gherkins	dill pickle
glacé cherries	candied cherries
green grapes	white grapes
hard-boiled eggs	hard-cooked eggs
haricot beans	navy beans
icing sugar	confectioner's sugar, or powered sugar
marrow	summer squash
pastry case	pie shell
plain chocolate	semi-sweet chocolate
plain flour	all-purpose flour
scampi	jumbo shrimp
scone	biscuit
self-raising flour	all-purpose flour with baking powder
single cream	coffee cream
sponge finger biscuits	lady fingers
spring onion	scallion
stock cube	bouillon cube
sultanas	seedless white rasins
swiss roll	jelly roll
tomato purée	tomato paste
unsalted butter	sweet butter
vanilla pod	vanilla bean
wholewheat flour	graham flour

TEMPERATURE CHECK

A reminder of the temperatures at which changes take place in water (at sea level) and sugar.

Water	Deg F	Deg C
freezes	32°	0°
simmers	115°	46°
scalds	130°	54°
boils	212°	100°
Sugar stage		
thread, for syrup	215°	101°
pearl, for jam, fondant sweets	220°	105°
soft ball, for soft fudge	240°	115°
hard ball, for hard fudge	260°	130°
crack, for soft toffee and frosting	280°	138°
hard crack, for hard toffee and spun sugar decorations	310°	155°
caramel, for praline and caramel coating	325°	170°

OVEN TEMPERATURE CHART

	Deg F	Deg C	Gas
Very cool	225	110	¼
	250	130	½
Cool	275	140	1
	300	150	2
Moderate	325	170	3
	350	180	4
Moderate-hot	375	190	5
	400	200	6
Hot	425	220	7
	450	230	8
Very hot	475	240	9

Note The temperatures of different makes and types of oven do vary. Consult the manufacturer's instructions to check the settings.

COOKING UTENSILS AND TERMS

British	American
baking tin	baking pan
biscuit dough	cookie dough
cake mixture	batter
cocktail stick	tooth pick
deep, loose-bottomed cake tin	spring-form pan
frying-pan	skillet
greaseproof paper	wax paper
grilled	broiled
kitchen paper	paper towel
liquidizer	blender
minced	ground
muslin	cheesecloth
pastry cutters	cookie cutters
patty tins	muffin pans
piping bag	pastry bag
sandwich tin	layer cake pan
skinned	pared
stoned	pitted
swiss roll tin	layer cake pan
to grill	to broil

MEASUREMENT GUIDE

Use this as a handy guide to convert metric, Imperial and American measures. British readers will note that American volume measures vary in weight conversion according to the ingredient – a cup of dried coconut, for example, weighs much less than a cup of sugar.

	Metric	Imperial	American
almonds, whole unblanched	175 g	6 oz	1 cup
apples, fresh, skinned and sliced	500 g	1 lb	3 cups
beans, green, fresh	500 g	1 lb	2½ cups
beans, kidney, dried	500 g	1 lb	2½ cups
beef, minced (ground)	500 g	1 lb	3 cups
butter	500 g	1 lb	2 cups or 4 sticks
cheese, hard	500 g	1 lb	4 cups
cheese, cottage	250 g	8 oz	2 cups
cheese, grated	125 g	4 oz	1 cup
chocolate	50 g	2 oz	2 squares
cocoa powder	500 g	1 lb	4 cups
coconut, desiccated	500 g	1 lb	5 cups
cornmeal	500 g	1 lb	3 cups
dates, stoned	500 g	1 lb	2½ cups
flour, white (all purpose)	500 g	1 lb	4 cups
flour, wholewheat (graham)	500 g	1 lb	3¾ cups
honey	500 g	1 lb	1⅓ cups
lard	500 g	1 lb	2 cups
macaroni, dry	500 g	1 lb	4½ cups
milk	600 ml	1 pint	2½ cups
mushrooms	250 g	8 oz	3 cups
oatmeal	500 g	1 lb	5⅓ cups
oil	450 ml	16 fl oz	2 cups
raisins, seedless	500 g	1 lb	2¾ cups
spaghetti, dry	500 g	1 lb	5½ cups
sugar, granulated	500 g	1 lb	2 cups
brown	500 g	1 lb	2¼ cups
caster (superfine)	500 g	1 lb	2 cups
icing (confectioner's)	500 g	1 lb	3½ cups
wheatgerm	500 g	1 lb	4 cups
yeast, fresh	15 g	½ oz	1 package
dry	15 ml	1 tbls	1 package

Note: An Imperial pint = approx 600 ml/20 fl oz
An American pint = approx 450 ml/16 fl oz, or 2 cups.

COOK'S NOTE

Readers are advised to follow either the metric or the Imperial measurements in each recipe. As the conversions are not exact, it is not possible to work from a combination of the two.

1: SOUPS

Since earliest times, soups have been served to make the most of local ingredients. A pot hanging over a camp fire would contain bones left over from spit-roast meat, dried pulses, grains, root vegetables, berries and "soup bunch" or its British equivalent, a bunch of pot herbs, for flavoring. The broth would get thicker and tastier as it was topped up with more ingredients each day and, with a chunk of bread, would be a meal in itself.

Old habits, especially when they produce a tasty and nourishing meal for very little trouble and expense, die hard. Many of the soups we enjoy today, particularly those with strong regional connections, bear a marked family likeness to the first cauldrons of *sup*.

Certainly the stock pot of meat, poultry or fish bones and flavoring vegetables is a direct descendant. When you have time, it is well worth making a batch of brown stock, chicken, fish and vegetable stocks and storing them in the freezer. They give "body" and that indefinable home-made flavor to your soups that no stock-in-a-cube ever can.

Soups have always been made from the best of what's available, whether it is in the wild, in the seas and rivers, on the farms, in the supermarkets or the larder. Philadelphia pepperpot, halfway between soup and stew, is a typical example, attributed to the ingenuity of General George Washington's cook, who concocted it from tripe, meat bones and spices in order to feed the soldiers. Later, it was sold on the streets of Philadelphia to a tempting street cry, "All hot! All hot! Pepper pot! Pepper pot! Makes back strong. Makes live long. All hot! Pepper pot!"

America's bountiful harvest has given rise to a wealth of delicious soups that can be served as a light lunch or supper dish, as a hearty meal or the appetizer to a contrasting main course. Enjoy a taste of the sea with Maryland crab soup, New England fish chowder and Manhattan clam chowder; the golden prairies with cream of corn soup topped with bobbing popcorn; the Deep South with chicken gumbo, thickened with okra, the descriptively sticky vegetable; vary the way you serve year-round dried pulses as the Settlers did, from warming black bean soup to tinglingly refreshing chilled mint and split pea soup; and come right up to date with blender soups to make in moments, with cream of Jerusalem artichoke or avocado and orange, both delightful choices to launch a dinner party.

All soups are more appetizing, even more nourishing, if served with a garnish. This can simply be a scattering of chopped herbs such as parsley, mint or chives; a spoonful of sunflower or pumpkin seeds, raisins or sultanas; chopped peanuts, pecans or almonds; cooked rice or pasta shapes; or whipped cream swirled on top and sprinkled with ground spices or chopped herbs. Crisply-fried croûtons can be tossed in herbs, spices, grated citrus fruit rinds or ground nuts for double flavor and texture value.

BROWN STOCK

Use brown stock for dark vegetable soups – for example, with red or black kidney beans or lentils, beetroot or onions, red meat soups such as oxtail and beef, and for consommé. You can, of course, substitute stock cubes and start your soups from there. But real home cooking was based on real home-made stock. Here's how it is done.

1 kg/2¼ lb beef bones,
   chopped small
15 ml/1 tbls beef dripping
1 large onion, sliced
2 medium carrots, sliced
4 celery stalks, sliced
45 ml/3 tbls mushroom stalks
   and peelings
a bunch of mixed herbs or a
   bouquet garni
5 ml/1 tsp salt
5 ml/1 tsp black peppercorns

In a large pan over moderate heat, fry the bones in the dripping, stirring frequently, until they are evenly brown. Add the vegetables and fry for a further 5 minutes, stirring once or twice.

Add 2.25 liters/4 pt water, cover the pan and bring slowly to the boil. Skim the foam from the top, add the herbs, season with salt and pepper and cover the pan. Bring to the boil and simmer for 3 hours, when the liquid volume should be reduced by one half.

Strain and discard the flavorings. Allow the stock to cool. When it is cold, lift off the solid layer of fat on the top.

Store in the refrigerator in covered containers for up to 1 week, or in the freezer.

CHICKEN STOCK

A versatile stock for use in root and green vegetable, corn and barley soups, and as a starting point for sauces and casseroles.

1 chicken carcass
1 large onion, sliced
2 medium carrots, sliced
4 celery stalks, sliced
1 bay leaf
5-6 parsley stalks
5 ml/1 tsp salt
5 ml/1 tsp black peppercorns

Put the carcass in a large pan, pour on 1.5 liters/2½ pt water, cover and bring slowly to the boil. Skim off the foam, add the remaining ingredients, cover and return to the boil. Simmer for 2½ hours, until the volume has reduced by about one half. Strain, discard the flavorings and cool the stock. Lift off the "lid" of fat and discard. Store in covered containers in the refrigerator for up to 1 week, or in the freezer.

VEGETABLE STOCK

For all vegetarian dishes and light vegetable soups.

25 g/l oz margarine
2 large onions, sliced
2 large carrots, sliced
6 celery stalks, sliced
1 large leek, sliced
1 small white turnip, sliced
a bunch of mixed herbs or a
   bouquet garni
5 ml/1 tsp salt
5 ml/1 tsp green peppercorns

Melt the margarine in a large pan over moderate heat and fry all the vegetables, stirring frequently, until they are soft but not changing color.

Add 2.25 liters/4 pt water, cover the pan and bring slowly to the boil. Skim any foam from the top, add the herbs and season with salt and pepper. Cover the pan, return to the boil and simmer for 3 hours. The stock should be reduced in volume by about one half.

Strain the stock, discarding the vegetables, and allow it to cool. Scrape the fat from the top. Store in covered containers in the refrigerator for up to 1 week, or in the freezer.

FISH STOCK

Use as the base for fish soups and chowders, sauces and casseroles.

1 kg/2¼ lb white fish
   trimmings; heads, tails,
   bones etc.
1 large onion, sliced
2 medium leeks, white part
   only, sliced
4 celery stalks, sliced
5-6 parsley stalks
2 bay leaves
30 ml/2 tbls cider vinegar
½ lemon, sliced
5 ml/1 tsp salt
5 ml/1 tsp black peppercorns
a pinch of cayenne pepper

Put the bones in a large pan, add 2.25 liters/4 pt water, cover and bring slowly to the boil. Skim off the foam, add the remaining ingredients, cover the pan and return to the boil. Simmer for 2 hours.

Strain through a colander lined with muslin or cheesecloth and discard all the ingredients. Cool, then store in covered containers in the refrigerator for up to 2 days, or in the freezer.

PHILADELPHIA PEPPERPOT SOUP

This dish is said to have been devised by General George Washington's cook during the War of Independence. With not much more than tripe and peppercorns in store, he produced a nourishing meal for the troops.

500 g/1 lb fresh honeycomb
    tripe, bought partly-cooked
1 kg/2¼ lb veal knucklebone
15 ml/1 tbls black
    peppercorns
2 *bouquets garnis* or a bunch of
    mixed fresh herbs
5 ml/1 tsp whole cloves
50 g/2 oz butter
3 large onions, thinly sliced
4 celery stalks, thinly sliced
2 medium carrots, thinly
    sliced
2 large potatoes, diced
2 medium beetroot, finely
    diced
50 g/2 oz long-grain rice
salt

Serves 8

Wash the tripe and cut it into small squares. Put it into a large pan with the veal knuckle and cover with 2 liters/3½ pt water. Cover the pan, bring to the boil and simmer for 15 minutes. Skim off the foam that rises to the top. Tie the herbs and spices in a piece of cheese cloth, add to the pan, cover and simmer for 3 hours.

Melt the butter in a pan and fry the onions, celery, carrots and potatoes over moderate heat for 5-6 minutes, stirring frequently. Add them to the large pan with the beetroot and rice. Cover, bring to the boil and simmer for 30 minutes or until the vegetables are tender. Remove the knuckle of veal, discard the skin and bone and cut the meat in cubes. Return the meat to the pan. Discard the bag of flavorings and season to taste with salt. Skim the fat from the surface of the soup before serving.

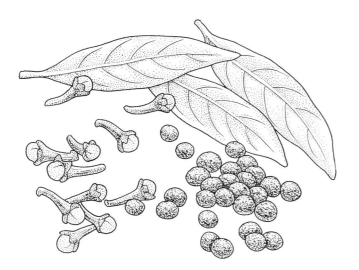

CHICKEN AND ALMOND CREAM SOUP

This is a "company" way to use left-over chicken.

1 liter/1¾ pt chicken stock
    (page 12)
250 g/8 oz cooked chicken,
    chopped
5-6 parsley stalks
1 bay leaf
1 medium onion, sliced
90 ml/6 tbls blanched
    almonds
600 ml/1 pt single cream
salt and pepper
45 ml/3 tbls blanched,
    slivered almonds, toasted,
    to garnish

Serves 6

Simmer the stock, chicken, parsley and onion in a covered pan for 15 minutes. Discard the parsley and bay leaf. Add the blanched almonds and liquidize in a blender or purée in a mouli-legumes. Return the purée to the pan, stir in the cream and season with salt and pepper. Reheat gently without boiling. Garnish with the toasted almonds.

MARYLAND CRAB SOUP

This is an adaptation of the regional dish, which uses she-crabs. Serve it with cracker biscuits.

25 g/l oz butter
1 small onion, finely chopped
2 celery stalks, finely chopped
30 ml/2 tbls flour
600 ml/1 pt milk, warm
450 ml/¾ pt single cream
150 ml/¼ pt dry sherry
375 g/12 oz fresh (or canned
    and drained) crab meat,
    finely diced
salt and pepper
2 hard-boiled eggs, sliced
15 ml/1 tbls chopped parsley
1 lemon, cut into 6 wedges

Serves 6

Melt the butter and fry the onion and celery over moderate heat for 3-4 minutes, stirring frequently. Stir in the flour to make a roux and then very gradually pour on the warm milk, stirring all the time. Bring to the boil, then simmer, stirring, for 3 minutes. Add the cream and sherry and heat gently, stirring to blend well.

Just before serving, stir in the crab meat and season to taste with salt and pepper. Garnish with the egg slices, sprinkled with parsley, and serve with a wedge of lemon.

MUSTARD SOUP

Photograph opposite

This recipe originally came from 14th-century France. In farming communities, especially, it has proved popular for the dash of spice it gives to the dairy produce.

25 g/1 oz butter
25 g/1 oz flour
600 ml/1 pt chicken stock
 (page 12), hot
300 ml/½ pt milk, hot
salt and pepper
1 small onion, grated
2 egg yolks
60 ml/4 tbls double cream
45 ml/3 tbls Meaux mustard
croûtons (page 16), to serve

Serves 4

Melt the butter and stir in the flour. Gradually pour on the stock and milk and whisk until smooth. Season with salt and pepper and stir in the onion juice collected beneath the grater (use the onion for another dish). Simmer for 10 minutes, then cool slightly.
 Beat together the egg yolks and cream and beat in a little of the soup. Stir into the pan, add the mustard, and whisk over very low heat for 1 minute. Serve hot, garnished with croûtons.

SOUTHERN CRAB SOUP

Photograph on page 10

50 g/2 oz butter
1 large onion, thinly sliced
450 g/15 oz can tomatoes
1.5 ml/¼ tsp cayenne pepper
1.5 ml/¼ tsp paprika
900 ml/1½ pt chicken stock
 (page 12)
300 g/10 oz can sweetcorn
 kernels, drained
500 g/1 lb crab meat, chopped
30 ml/2 tbls chopped parsley
salt and pepper

Serves 6

Melt the butter and fry the onion for 3-4 minutes over moderate heat, stirring once or twice. Add the tomatoes with their juice from the can, the cayenne and paprika. Cover and simmer for 5 minutes. Add the stock, sweetcorn, and crab meat, cover and simmer for 3 minutes. Stir in the parsley and season with salt and pepper. Serve with plenty of crusty bread.

CABBAGE BORSCHT

To do justice to this Jewish version of an East European soup, make it the day before to allow the flavors to harmonize. It is especially good served with rye bread.

1 small white cabbage,
   shredded
salt
375 g/12 oz brisket of beef
1 marrow bone, chopped
1.5 liters/2¾ pt brown stock
   (page 12)
1 medium onion, finely
   chopped
450 g/15 oz can tomatoes
15 ml/1 tbls sugar
pepper
60 ml/4 tbls sweet sherry
30 ml/2 tbls lemon juice
60 ml/4 tbls sultanas

Serves 8

Put the cabbage into a colander over a dish and sprinkle with salt.
   Put the brisket, bone and stock into a pan and bring slowly to the boil. Skim the foam from the surface. Add the onion, tomatoes and sugar and season with pepper. Cover the pan and simmer for 2 hours.
   Rinse the cabbage under cold running water to remove the salt, and blanch it for 2 minutes in boiling water. Drain it thoroughly.
   Discard the bones. Lift the meat from the pan and cut it into bite-sized pieces. Return to the pan, add the cabbage, cover and bring to the boil. Simmer for 30 minutes. Add the sherry, lemon juice and sultanas, taste and adjust seasoning if needed. Simmer for 5 minutes.

NEW ORLEANS ONION SOUP

Americans have adopted this classic warm brown soup as their own. Good stock makes all the difference.

40 g/1½ oz butter
500 g/l lb onions, sliced
1 liter/1¾ pt brown stock
   (page 12)
150 ml/¼ pt dry sherry
salt and pepper
6×1-cm/½-in slices cut from
   French loaf
125 g/4 oz Gruyère cheese,
   grated

Serves 6

Melt the butter and fry the onions over moderate heat for 8-10 minutes, stirring frequently, until they are soft and light brown. Pour on the stock, bring to the boil, cover and simmer for 20 minutes. Add the sherry, season with salt and pepper and simmer for 10 minutes.
   Toast the bread on both sides. Pour the soup into a flameproof serving bowl, float the bread on top and sprinkle with the cheese. Broil until the cheese is bubbly and serve at once.

ST. LUCIA PUMPKIN SOUP

Photograph on page 17

This golden-yellow soup with just a hint of spice is extra good served with muffins or scones

25 g/1 oz butter
500 g/1 lb prepared pumpkin,
   diced
250 g/8 oz carrots, sliced
1 small onion, sliced
1.5 ml/¼ tsp ground mace
750 ml/1½ pt chicken stock
   (page 12)
a pinch of grated nutmeg
300 ml/½ pt single cream
salt and pepper
60 ml/4 tbls whipped cream,
   to garnish

Serves 4

Melt the butter and fry the pumpkin, carrots and onion over moderate heat for 3-4 minutes, stirring occasionally. Add the mace and nutmeg and stir for 1 minute. Pour on the stock, bring to the boil, cover and simmer for 20 minutes.
   Liquidize the soup in a blender or rub through a sieve. Return to the pan, stir in the cream and season with salt and pepper. Reheat gently. Garnish each bowl with the whipped cream sprinkled with a small pinch of mace or nutmeg.

CHILLED AVOCADO AND ORANGE SOUP

The tang of citrus fruit is perfect with the subtle blandness of avocado.

1 large avocado, halved,
   stoned, peeled and sliced
1 small onion, sliced
450 ml/¾ pt chicken stock
   (page 12)
125 g/4 oz can frozen
   concentrated orange juice,
   thawed
150 ml/¼ pt single cream
salt and pepper
15 ml/1 tbls chopped chives,
   to garnish
4 thin slices orange

Serves 4

Put the avocado into a pan with the onion and stock, bring to the boil, cover and simmer for 5 minutes. Liquidize in a blender or rub through a sieve. Cool, then stir in the orange juice and cream and season to taste with salt and pepper. Chill in the refrigerator until serving in chilled bowls. Garnish each serving with chives and a slice of orange. For a touch of luxury, stand the bowls in larger ones filled with cracked ice.

CHICKEN GUMBO SOUP

A hearty Southern soup which you could serve, farmhouse style, as the main course for an informal lunch party.

50 g/2 oz butter
1 boiling fowl, about 1.5 kg/
   3½ lb, chopped into pieces
45 ml/3 tbls flour
500 g/1 lb canned tomatoes
250 g/8 oz okra, sliced
250 g/8 oz frozen corn kernels
1 green pepper, seeded and
   sliced
1 large onion, sliced
50 g/2 oz long-grain rice
30 ml/2 tbls fine semolina
salt and pepper

Serves 8-12

Melt the butter in a large pan. Toss the chicken pieces in the flour and fry them in the butter over moderate heat for 10 minutes, turning them often. Pour on enough water to cover the chicken – about 1 liter/1¾ pt – and bring to the boil.

   Skim the foam from the top, cover and simmer for 1¾ hours, or until the meat falls from the bone. Strain and reserve the stock. Discard the bones and cut the meat into small pieces.

   Place all the vegetables and the rice in the pan, stir in the semolina and gradually pour on 1 liter/1¾ pt water, still stirring. Bring to the boil and simmer for 30 minutes or until all the vegetables are tender. Stir in the reserved chicken stock and meat, season with salt and pepper and heat thoroughly.

MANHATTAN CLAM CHOWDER

The Manhattan version of this tasty and filling soup contains tomatoes; its Boston rival does not. The chowder is best made a day in advance, and reheated.

125 g/4 oz salt pork, rinded
   and finely diced
4 celery stalks, thinly sliced
500 g/1 lb onions, thinly sliced
500 g/1 lb potatoes, diced
750 g/1½ lb canned tomatoes,
   chopped
2×500 g/1 lb bottled clams
2.5 ml/½ tsp dried thyme
30 ml/2 tbls chopped parsley
salt and pepper
5 ml/1 tsp white wine vinegar

Serves 6-8

Fry the pork cubes in a non-stick pan and discard the meat. Fry the celery and onions in the pork fat for about 4 minutes over moderate heat. Add the potatoes, tomatoes and juice from the can, bring to the boil and cover. Simmer for 20 minutes. Drain the clams, reserving the juice. Chop the clams and add them to the pan with the juice, thyme and parsley. Bring slowly to simmering point, season to taste with salt and pepper, add the vinegar and serve at once, or cool and reheat gently the following day. Do not boil the soup once you have added the clams.

NEW ENGLAND FISH CHOWDER

For the subtle and authentic flavor of this traditional East Coast soup, salt pork is essential. Make the soup a day in advance so that the flavors can blend.

750 ml/1½ pt fish stock (page
   12)
1 kg/2¼ lb white fish fillets,
   such as haddock, cod, coley
175 g/6 oz salt pork, rinded
   and diced
1 large onion, chopped
225 g/8 oz potatoes, peeled
600 ml/1 pt milk
300 ml/½ pt dry cider
salt and pepper
40 g/1½ oz butter, diced
30 ml/2 tbls chopped parsley

Serves 8

Cook the fish in the stock for 10 minutes, then drain, reserving the stock. Remove the skin and any bones, cut the fish into large bite-sized pieces and set aside.

   Fry the pork in a non-stick pan until the fat runs. Remove the meat with a draining spoon and set it aside. Fry the onions in the fat for 3-4 minutes over moderate heat, stirring frequently. Stir in the potatoes, pour on the fish stock, bring to the boil, cover and simmer for 15 minutes. Stir in the milk and cider, season with salt and pepper and heat gently without boiling. Add the fish and heat very gently. Carefully stir in the pork. Add the butter and sprinkle on the parsley. Serve very hot.

VIRGINIA PEANUT SOUP

Peanuts were grown largely in Virginia and North Carolina until the Civil War. Now they are a widely grown and highly versatile commercial crop.

25 g/1 oz butter
1 medium onion, sliced
1 medium carrot, chopped
30 ml/2 tbls flour
600 ml/1 pt chicken stock
  (page 12)
125 g/4 oz unsalted peanuts,
  skinned
60 ml/4 tbls peanut butter
150 ml/¼ pt single cream
60 ml/4 tbls medium sherry
salt and pepper
15 ml/1 tbls chopped parsley

Serves 4

Melt the butter and fry the onion and carrot over moderate heat for 3-4 minutes, stirring frequently. Stir in the flour and gradually pour on the stock, stirring constantly. Add the peanuts, bring to the boil, cover and simmer for 40 minutes.

   Liquidize in a blender or push through a mouli-legumes to make a purée. Return to the pan, add the peanut butter, cream and sherry. Season with salt and pepper and heat gently without boiling. Garnish with the parsley.

MONTANA BARLEY SOUP

Both the barley and pulses become well-flavored with the meat and vegetables. Serve in shallow plates with plenty of crusty bread.

1.5 kg/3½ lb meaty beef
  bones, chopped
2 marrow bones, chopped
150 g/5 oz pearl barley
150 g/5 oz split green peas
1 large onion
4 whole cloves
4 celery stalks, halved
4 medium carrots, halved
5-6 parsley stalks
2 bay leaves
salt and pepper

Serves 6

Put the bones in a pan with 2.25 liters/4 pt water and bring slowly to the boil. Skim off the foam, cover and simmer for 1 hour. Add the barley, peas, vegetables and herbs and simmer for 2 hours.

   Lift out the bones and vegetables with a straining spoon and discard the vegetables. Cut the meat from the bones and return the meat to the pan. Season with salt and pepper. Allow the soup to cool, then chill overnight in the refrigerator. Lift off the lid of fat. Reheat the soup and adjust seasoning if necessary.

BLACK BEAN SOUP

This soup makes a meal in itself, and is interestingly full of contrasting textures and flavors.

75 g/3 oz dried black beans*,
  soaked overnight and
  drained
100 g/4 oz streaky bacon,
  rinded and chopped
1 large onion, sliced
1 large carrot, thinly sliced
375 g/12 oz red cabbage,
  shredded
1 liter/1¾ pt brown stock
  (page 12)
½ small cauliflower, broken
  into florets
salt and pepper
15 ml/1 tbsp lemon juice
grated Parmesan cheese, to
  garnish

Serves 6-8

Fry the bacon and onion in a pan over moderate heat for 4-5 minutes, stirring frequently. Stir in the carrot and cook for 2 minutes. Add the cabbage and beans, pour on the stock and stir well. Bring to the boil and boil for 10 minutes. Cover the pan and simmer for 1½ hours.

   Add the cauliflower, season with salt and pepper and simmer for 45 minutes, or until the beans and vegetables are tender. Stir in the lemon juice, taste and adjust seasoning if needed. Sprinkle with cheese just before serving.

*Other dried pulses such as red kidney beans, haricot or pinto beans may be substituted for the black beans.

2:FISH AND SEAFOODS

America's history seems to be woven around her shores. No present-day fisherman's tales can ever match early accounts for superlatives and incredibility.

Back in the 16th century, the Vikings fished the Eastern Coast at their leisure, long before the Continent had been "discovered." Once it had, and the Pilgrims had landed, international communication really got under way, and we come across "walking on the water" accounts. Or, more specifically, tales of Settlers strolling across Plymouth Bay on the backs of the fish shoals, as if they were so many stepping-stones. The pity of it is, at that point they hadn't actually learned to catch fish.

Squanto, the native who was friendly, showed them how to pick up eels with their hands. And when they also caught cod, the "Cape Cod turkey," they raised an effigy to it in Massachusetts. Salmon swam up-river every sring from the East Coast to spawn, and the Settlers laid down a plentiful supply, salted and pickled, to last the winter.

It may be an exaggeration, but persistent legend has it that there were lobsters big enough to feed four hungry men, and a French traveler insisted that trout, to be found in every lake and stream, were quite as big as a man's thigh. And tasty, too.

Maryland and Virginia have always arguably boasted the best oysters in the world, and in such quantity that imagination ran riot in devising ways to cook them. Our recipe for oyster fritters survives from those early origins, whilst Oyster Rockefeller shows what a good restaurant can do to a crustacean. Alongside oysters come the clams, which offered themselves for boiling, steaming, broiling, braising, saucing-up with tomatoes and spices, disguising under pie crusts and popping into soups and casseroles – not to mention chowder (page 18). The British image of an American on holiday tends to center on a clam bake, which is another thing the Indians taught their colonizers, and is explored further in Chapter 4.

It is the Dungeness crab that is the toast of the Pacific, served broiled, baked, cold with mayonnaise or however. Our recipes for Maryland crab cakes and crab soufflé bring a taste of the ocean to enthusiasts, even if they have to acquire it by courtesy of the supermarket.

The Hudson River flowed with shad, a fish that might be described (inaccurately) as a big cousin of the herring and mackerel. Delicate though the fish itself is, shad is most prized for the hard roe, which makes a quite inimitable sauce (see recipe on page 30). As for herring from the North Atlantic, George Washington liked them so much he is said to have enjoyed them for breakfast, with corn cakes.

Florida, at the last count, had 4 million acres of water, much of it inland, so the shrimps, prawns, mackerel, mullet, flounder, red snapper, perch and bream have a largish swimming pool. Fifty percent of California's fishing industry is accounted for by tuna, that most versatile of fish, with sole, sardine, squid, mackerel and salmon sharing the rest.

These recipes, in so short a space, bring only a glimpse of one of America's most exciting harvests.

SPAGHETTI WITH CLAM SAUCE

Photograph on page 20

Rumor has it that this is Barry Manilow's favorite dish - which seems as good a reason as any for trying it.

350 g/12 oz spaghetti
salt
40 g/1½ oz butter
15 ml/1 tbls vegetable oil
1 medium onion, finely
   chopped
300 g/10 oz can clams, drained
   and rinsed
2 × 150 g/5 oz cans tomato
   purée
5 ml/1 tsp dried tarragon
60 ml/4 tbls dry sherry
pepper

Serves 4

Cook the spaghetti in boiling, salted water for 10 minutes, or until it is just tender to the bite. Drain, refresh it in cold water and drain again. Toss with the butter and keep warm.

Meanwhile, heat the oil in a pan and fry the onion for 3-4 minutes, stirring occasionally. Stir in the clams, tomato purée, tarragon and 60 ml/4 tbls water and simmer for 5 minutes. Stir in the sherry, season well with pepper and heat through.

Turn the spaghetti into a heated dish and top with the sauce.

MARINATED FISH KEBABS

Photograph on page 25

A whole new flavor is imparted to the fish before it is grilled with colorful fruit and vegetables. Use chunks of white fish as an alternative to mackerel.

3 medium mackerel, cleaned
   and cut into 4-cm/1½-in
   slices
2 medium onions, sliced into
   rings
4 small courgettes, sliced
1 lemon, thinly sliced
Marinade
45 ml/3 tbls clear honey
30 ml/2 tbls lemon juice
15 ml/1 tbls orange juice
15 ml/1 tbls soy sauce
a few drops of Tabasco sauce

Serves 4

Heat the marinade ingredients and stir to dissolve the honey. Bring to the boil, then cool.

Thread the fish, vegetables and lemon on 4 skewers, lay them on a flat dish and pour over the marinade. Baste and turn the skewers occasionally and leave for 1 hour.

Cook the skewers under medium grill for 15 minutes, turning them regularly and basting them with any remaining sauce. Serve on a bed of rice.

CALIFORNIA SALMON STEAKS

This is one of those dishes that is a stand-by of busy cooks – it is high on appeal and low on labor!

6 salmon steaks, about 2.5 cm/
   1 in thick
Marinade
90 ml/6 tbls vegetable oil
75 ml/5 tbls orange juice
15 ml/1 tbls lemon juice
5 ml/1 tsp grated orange rind
1 small onion, sliced
a few parsley stalks
5 ml/1 tsp soy sauce
salt and pepper
Sauce
1 large avocado
125 g/4 oz unsalted butter,
   softened
10 ml/2 tsp orange juice
5 ml/1 tsp grated orange rind
2-3 drops Worcestershire
   sauce

Serves 6

Arrange the salmon steaks in a shallow dish. Mix together all the ingredients for the marinade, pour them over the salmon, cover and leave in the refrigerator for 3-4 hours, turning the steaks frequently.

Beat the butter until it is smooth. Halve, stone and peel the avocado, mash the flesh and beat it into the butter. Gradually beat in the orange juice, a few drops at a time, then the orange rind and Worcestershire sauce. Season with salt and pepper. Shape into a roll, cover with foil and chill.

Drain the salmon steaks and cook them under a moderately hot grill for 4-5 minutes on each side, or until the flesh is just firm.

Serve the steaks garnished with pats of the avocado butter.

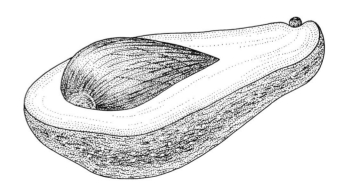

KEDGEREE

Photograph on page 24

Here is a dish that originated in India, as *kitchri*, and has traveled all round the world, finding a home wherever hearty appetites and seafoods come together.

175 g/6 oz long-grain rice
salt
50 g/2 oz butter
500 g/1 lb smoked haddock
    fillet
1 bay leaf
5 ml/1 tsp black peppercorns
a few parsley stalks
2 eggs, lightly beaten
15 ml/1 tbls chopped parsley
a pinch of cayenne pepper
4 hard-boiled eggs, quartered
    and sliced

Serves 4

Cook the rice in boiling, salted water for 12 minutes, or until it is just tender. Drain, refresh it in cold water, drain again thoroughly and return it to the pan. Toss the rice in half the butter and keep warm.

Cook the fish in boiling water (or milk and water) with the bay leaf and peppercorns for 10 minutes. Drain it, remove the skin and any bones and flake the fish.

Stir the fish and the remaining butter into the rice and heat very gently. Stir in the beaten eggs and parsley and season with cayenne. Lastly, stir in the chopped eggs and serve at once.

Triangles of toast and creamed leaf spinach are good accompaniments.

TWICE-COOKED HADDOCK WITH CREAM

Haddock is not the prerogative of the Scots – it is just as familiar off the shores of America. This is an old East Coast way of serving it.

4 fillets smoked haddock,
    about 175g/6oz each
1 small onion, halved
6 black peppercorns
a few parsley stalks
40 g/1½ oz butter, diced
freshly-ground black pepper
300 ml/½ pt double cream
parsley sprigs, to garnish

Serves 4

Put the fish in a shallow pan with the onion, peppercorns and parsley stalks. Cover with water, bring to the boil and simmer for 5 minutes. Drain and dry the fish thoroughly.

Place the fish in a greased shallow flameproof dish and dot with the butter. Grind plenty of pepper over the fish and cook under a moderate grill for 5 minutes, basting it frequently with the butter. Gently heat the cream, without boiling it.

Pour the cream over the fish, garnish with the parsley and serve with boiled potatoes.

BAKED FILLETS WITH HERB BUTTER

8 small fillets of plaice, or
    other white fish
25 g/1 oz butter
4 rashers streaky bacon, rind
    removed, finely chopped
50 g/2 oz mushrooms,
    chopped
90 ml/6 tbls canned
    sweetcorn, drained
60 ml/4 tbls breadcrumbs
salt and pepper
60 ml/4 tbls dry cider
Herb butter
125 g/4 oz unsalted butter,
    softened
5 ml/1 tsp lemon juice
15 ml/1 tbls chopped parsley
15 ml/1 tbls chopped chives
1 clove garlic, crushed
30 ml/2 tbls chopped canned
    pimento

Serves 4

Melt the butter and fry the bacon, mushrooms and sweetcorn over moderate heat for 4 minutes, stirring frequently. Remove from the heat, season with salt and pepper and stir in the breadcrumbs.

Place the fish fillets skin side down and divide the filling between them. Roll up the fish and secure with fine twine or wooden cocktail sticks. Arrange the rolls in a greased baking dish, pour over the cider and cover with a lid or foil. Bake in the oven at 190C/375F/gas 5 for 15 minutes.
Herb butter

Beat the butter until it is smooth, then beat in the lemon juice a few drops at a time. Beat in the remaining ingredients. Shape into a roll, cover with foil and chill. This can be done well in advance.

Remove the ties or sticks and serve the fish with pats of the herb butter.

COD CATALAN

Photograph on page 28.

The cod combines with the culinary influence of the Spanish to make a delightfully fiery fish dish.

25 g/1 oz butter
1 large onion, sliced
2 cloves garlic, crushed
2 celery stalks, thinly sliced
25 g/1 oz flour
1.5 ml/¼ tsp cayenne pepper
1 red pepper, seeded and
    chopped
450 g/15 oz can tomatoes
60 ml/4 tbls dry white wine
15 ml/1 tbls tomato purée
50 g/2 oz stuffed olives,
    halved
4 cod steaks, about 175 g/6 oz
    each
15 ml/1 tbls lemon juice
salt and pepper
50 g/2 oz hazelnuts, chopped
30 ml/2 tbls chopped parsley

Serves 4

Melt the butter and fry the onion, garlic and celery over moderate heat for 3 minutes, stirring once or twice. Stir in the flour and cayenne, then the red pepper, tomatoes, the tomato juice from the can, the wine and the tomato purée. Bring the sauce to the boil, stirring. Stir in the olives.

Pour the sauce into a shallow baking dish. Sprinkle the fish with lemon juice and season it with salt and pepper. Place the fish in the sauce, and cover the dish. Bake in the oven at 190C/375F/gas 5 for 25 minutes. Garnish with the nuts and parsley.

FISH CRESPOLINI

The Italian influence means wafer-thin pancakes with dreamy fillings – such as fish, and shellfish, and colorful vegetables, and cheese, and cream, and ...

1 recipe Pancakes (page 120)
375 g/12 oz white fish fillet,
    such as cod
200 ml/7 fl oz milk
1 bay leaf
6 black peppercorns
a few parsley stalks
25 g/1 oz butter
25 g/1 oz flour
300 ml/½ pt single cream
salt and pepper
125 g/4 oz cooked peeled
    prawns
a pinch of cayenne pepper
2 canned pimentos, drained
    and chopped
5 ml/1 tsp lemon juice
75 g/3 oz grated Parmesan
    cheese

Serves 6

Make the pancakes as directed on page 120.

Cook the fish in the milk with the bay leaf, peppercorns and parsley for 5 minutes. Strain and reserve the liquor. Skin the fish, remove any bones, and flake it.

Melt the butter and stir in the flour. Gradually pour on the fish liquor, stirring all the time. Simmer for 3 minutes. Add the cream, season with salt and pepper and bring just to boiling point, stirring.

Divide the sauce into two equal parts. Into one half, stir the fish, prawns, cayenne, pimentos and lemon juice. Fill the pancakes with this mixture, roll them up and arrange them in a greased ovenproof dish.

Stir two-thirds of the cheese into the remaining sauce and pour it over the pancakes. Sprinkle the rest of the cheese on top. Cook under a moderately hot grill for 5-7 minutes, until the sauce is brown and bubbling.

TROUT VINAIGRETTE

This delicious and subtle blend of flavors was brought to the USA by the German immigrants and is reminiscent of the old way of pickling fish. It's a perfect "company" way to serve this delicate fish.

4 medium trout, cleaned
50 g/2 oz butter
1 medium onion, sliced into
    rings
½ green pepper, seeded and
    sliced into rings
60 ml/4 tbls single cream
10 ml/2 tsp cider vinegar
salt and pepper
2 hard-boiled eggs, finely
    chopped

Serves 4

Melt half the butter in a large frying-pan and fry the onion and pepper rings for 3-4 minutes over moderate heat, turning them once. Remove from the pan and melt the remaining butter.

Fry the trout for 6 minutes on each side and transfer to a heated serving dish. Add the cream and vinegar to the pan, stir well and season the sauce with salt and pepper. Do not allow to boil. Pour the sauce over the fish, scatter the onion and pepper rings on top and garnish with the chopped egg.

POACHED RED SNAPPER WITH SHRIMP SAUCE

Red snapper is considered to be one of the best catches in the Gulf, and is always delectable whether served fried, broiled or baked. This recipe acknowledges the French influence in the Southern States.

1×2-kg/4½-lb red snapper,
   cleaned
10 ml/2 tsp rock salt
a few parsley stalks
½ lemon, sliced
2 small onions, halved
Sauce
60 ml/4 tbls orange juice
8 peppercorns
2 egg yolks
125 g/4 oz butter, diced
5 ml/1 tsp grated orange rind
salt and pepper
250 g/8 oz cooked peeled
   shrimps

Serves 6

Wrap the fish in a piece of muslin or cheesecloth and lay it in a fish kettle or roasting pan. Cover the fish with water and add the salt, parsley, lemon and onions. Bring to the boil and simmer very gently over low heat for 30-35 minutes. (Calculate the cooking time at 8 minutes per 500 g/1 lb.)

Meanwhile, make the sauce. Put the orange juice and peppercorns into a small pan and boil to reduce the liquid by half. Strain it into the top of a double boiler or a bowl fitted over a pan of simmering water. Whisk in the egg yolks and add the butter piece by piece, whisking all the time. Stir in the orange rind and season with salt and pepper. Stir in the shrimps and allow just to heat through.

Transfer the fish to a heated serving dish, garnish it with a little of the sauce and serve the rest separately. Serve with boiled new potatoes and a green salad.

CRISPY COD WITH PAPRIKA SAUCE

The early travelers found the seas around America so thick with this succulent fish that Cape Cod was named in honor of it. Here is a refinement of the familiar batter-fried fish.

1 kg/2¼ lb fresh cod fillet
6 rashers streaky bacon, rind
   removed, cut into small
   squares
oil, for frying
Marinade
45 ml/3 tbls vegetable oil
45 ml/3 tbls lemon juice
15 ml/1 tbls orange juice
5 ml/1 tsp grated orange rind
salt and pepper
Batter
125 g/4 oz flour
salt
45 ml/3 tbls vegetable oil
200 ml/7 fl oz lukewarm water
1 large egg white
Sauce
150 ml/¼ pt soured cream
1 small onion, finely chopped
10 ml/2 tsp lemon juice
2.5 ml/½ tsp paprika

Serves 4

Skin the fish, remove any bones and cut into 4-cm/1 ½-in pieces. Mix together the marinade ingredients, pour over the fish and toss well. Cover and leave in the refrigerator for 3 hours, turning occasionally.

To make the batter, sift the flour and salt, stir in the oil and gradually beat in the water. Just before using, stiffly whisk the egg white and fold it into the batter.

Mix together the ingredients for the sauce, season with salt and pepper and set aside. To make in advance and store, cover and keep in the refrigerator.

Drain the fish from the marinade and pat it dry. Heat about 4 cm/1 ½ in oil in a pan until it is just smoking. Dip the fish in the batter, drain off any excess and fry a few pieces at a time in the hot oil. Drain, toss on kitchen paper and keep warm while you fry the remainder.

Fry the bacon without fat in a non-stick pan.

Serve the fish garnished with the bacon, and the sauce separately.

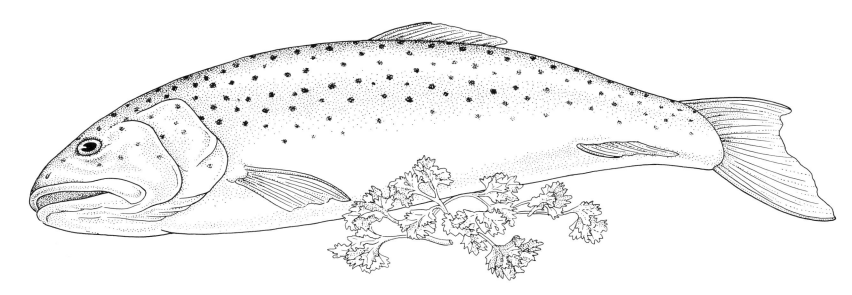

FISH AND HAM ROLLS

Photograph on page 29

Fried fish with a tasty difference – rolled with ham and spices.

4×250 g/8 oz fillets plaice,
    skinned and halved
    lengthways
1 egg yolk
15 ml/1 tbls mustard powder
5 ml/1 tsp white vinegar
2.5 ml/½ tsp ground turmeric
2.5 ml/½ tsp dried thyme
salt and pepper
flour, for dusting
125 g/4 oz thinly-sliced ham
1 orange, sliced, to garnish
Batter
75 g/3 oz flour
15 ml/1 tbls vegetable oil
1 egg white, stiffly whisked
oil, for deep frying

Serves 4

Mix together the egg yolk, mustard, vinegar, turmeric and thyme and season with salt and pepper. Lightly dust the fish with flour and spread the mustard paste on the inside. Cut the ham slices to shape and place on top of the paste. Roll up each fillet to enclose the ham and secure with a cocktail stick.

To make the batter, sift the flour with a pinch of salt and beat in the oil. Gradually beat in 150 ml/¼ pt water and beat until smooth. Just before using, fold in the egg white.

Heat about 4 cm/1½ in oil in a deep pan to a temperature of 180C/360F. Dip the fish rolls in the batter, draining off the excess. Fry them in the oil for 8-10 minutes, until they are golden brown. Drain the fish and toss on kitchen paper to dry. Serve hot, garnished with the orange segments.

HALIBUT AND MUSHROOM PARCELS

Halibut is recognised as one of the finest catches of the American fishing industry. This is an updated version of the "en papillotte" method of cooking.

4 halibut steaks, about 2.5 cm/
    1 in thick
125 g/4 oz button
    mushrooms, sliced
25 g/1 oz butter, diced
4 spring onions, thinly sliced
salt and pepper
5 ml/1 tsp curry powder
30 ml/2 tbls white wine
150 ml/¼ pt double cream

Serves 4

Cut 4 squares of foil large enough to enclose the fish steaks. Grease the foil and place a fish steak in the center of each. Draw up the sides of the foil to make a dish shape. Divide the butter, mushrooms and onions between each parcel, season with salt and pepper and the curry powder and pour over the wine and cream. Seal the parcels securely.

Place the parcels on a baking sheet and cook in the oven at 190C/375F/gas 5 for 20 minutes. Serve in the foil parcels.

SHAD WITH ANCHOVY SAUCE

Shad, native to the Atlantic seaboard and successfully introduced to the waters of the West Coast, can be likened to herring, though it is much larger. The roe is considered a delicacy and is served as a sauce with many other fish species.

1 × 1.5-kg/3½-lb shad with
    roe, cleaned, boned and
    split
salt and pepper
125 g/4 oz butter
200 ml/7 fl oz dry white wine
20 ml/4 tsp flour
150 ml/¼ pt chicken stock
    (page 12)
5 ml/1 tsp anchovy paste
15 ml/1 tbls lemon juice
150 ml/¼ pt double cream
2 egg yolks
parsley sprigs, to garnish

Serves 4-6

Put the shad roe in a greased baking dish and prick the membrane with a needle. Season with salt and pepper and dot with one-third of the butter. Pour on the wine, cover and bake in the oven at 180C/350F/gas 4 for 35 minutes.

Place the shad, skin side down on a greased baking dish. Season with salt and pepper and dot with half the remaining butter. Cook in the oven for 30 minutes, basting the fish frequently with the pan juices.

In a small pan, melt the remaining butter and stir in the flour. Pour on the liquor from the roe, and the stock, stirring all the time. Stir in the anchovy paste and simmer the sauce for 4 minutes. Remove the membrane from the roe. Mash the roe and stir it into the sauce with the lemon juice. Beat together the cream and egg yolks and beat them into the sauce. Taste and adjust seasoning if necessary. Do not allow the sauce to boil.

Serve the fish garnished with a little sauce and with the parsley, and serve the rest of the sauce separately.

New potatoes and leaf spinach are good accompaniments.

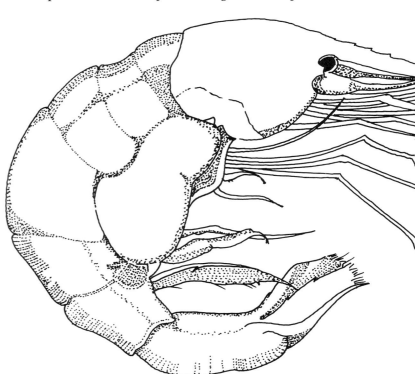

STIR-FRIED PRAWNS

Oriental influences have shown Americans tasty ways to serve their shellfish. This way couldn't be simpler.

750 g/1½ lb large prawns, in
   shell
60 ml/4 tbls peanut oil
5-cm/2-in piece fresh ginger
   root, peeled and finely
   chopped
1 clove garlic, finely chopped
2 spring onions, thinly sliced
10-cm/4-in piece cucumber,
   skinned, seeded and finely
   diced
Sauce
45 ml/3 tbls dry sherry
45 ml/3 tbls soy sauce
15 ml/1 tbls clear honey
5 ml/1 tsp cornflour
a large pinch of salt

Serves 4

First mix together the ingredients for the sauce and set aside.

Trim the prawns, leaving the shells on. Heat the oil in a large frying-pan or wok. Stir-fry the ginger, garlic and onions over moderate heat for 1 minute. Add the prawns and stir-fry for 1 minute.

Pour on the sauce and simmer for 4 minutes. Scatter with the cucumber and serve at once with boiled rice.

Offer fingerbowls for sticky fingers. Float a single white flower or a thin slice of lemon in each.

PRAWN PÂTÉ

This decorative dish freezes perfectly, so you can make it in advance for a first course or a light lunch.

500 g/1 lb fresh cod or
   haddock
300 ml/½ pt milk
1 bay leaf
salt and pepper
50 g/2 oz butter
40 g/1½ oz flour
300 ml/½ pt single cream
15 g/½ oz powdered gelatine
45 ml/3 tbls white wine
30 ml/2 tbls horseradish
   mustard
15 ml/1 tbls lemon juice
250 g/8 oz cooked peeled
   prawns
1.5 ml/¼ tsp ground mace
150 ml/¼ pt double cream,
   whipped
6 stuffed olives, sliced
1 bunch watercress sprigs, to
   garnish

Serves 6

Simmer the fish in the milk with a bay leaf, salt and pepper for 10 minutes. Strain and reserve the liquor. Skin the fish, remove any bones and cut the fish into pieces.

Melt the butter, stir in the flour and gradually pour on the fish liquor and the cream, stirring all the time. Stir until thickened, then simmer for 3 minutes. Remove from heat. Dissolve the gelatine in the wine. Stir it into the sauce with the mustard, lemon juice, fish and half the prawns. Season with salt, pepper and mace. Liquidize in a blender or food processor and set aside to cool completely.

Fold in the cream and check seasoning. Pour the mixture into an oiled 1.25 liter/2 pt fish-shaped or other mold and level the surface. Chill for at least 3 hours.

Turn out the mold on to a flat dish. If using a fish mold, place a slice of olive to represent the eye. Toss together the remaining prawns, the olives and watercress and arrange them around the mold.

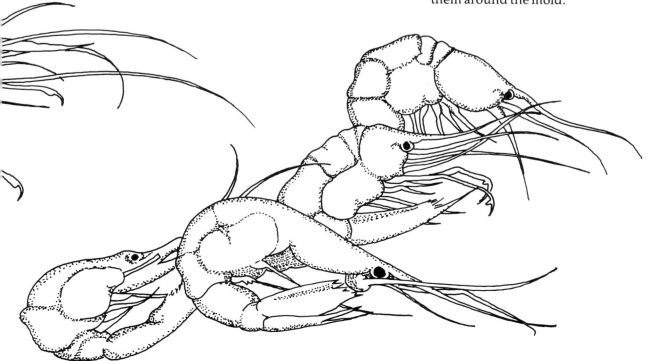

SLIMMERS' BRAN FLAN

Photograph opposite

In line with today's health kick, a flan that is high in fiber, low in calories, and great to taste!

150 g/5 oz wholewheat flour
75 g/3 oz low-fat spread
25 g/1 oz bran buds
salt
Filling
500 g/1 lb cottage cheese,
   sieved
1 thin celery stalk, finely
   chopped
30 ml/2 tbls chopped
   cucumber
4 spring onions, finely
   chopped
175 g/6 oz shelled prawns
pepper
1.5 ml/¼ tsp cayenne pepper
1 green pepper, seeded and
   sliced into rings
a sprig of parsley, to garnish

Serves 4

Put the flour in a bowl, rub in the spread and stir in the bran and salt. Sprinkle on just enough water to make a firm dough. On a lightly-floured board, roll out the dough and use to line a 20-cm/8-in flan case. Cover the base with foil and baking beans and bake "blind" in the oven at 200C/400F/gas 6 for 20 minutes. Remove the beans and foil and cook the pastry case for a further 5 minutes. Cool on a wire rack.

Stir the celery, cucumber, onions and prawns into the cheese and season with salt, pepper and cayenne. Spoon the filling into the pastry case. Arrange the pepper rings on top and garnish with the parsley.

CHARLESTON SHRIMP PIE

From pre-Colonial days, this recipe from South Carolina makes homely use of the abundant sea harvest.

8×12-mm/¼-in slices cut
    from a large white loaf,
    crusts removed, and diced
1 bay leaf
300 ml/½ pt milk
50g/2oz unsalted butter,
    melted
5 large eggs, beaten
1 green pepper, seeded and
    finely chopped
6 spring onions, thinly sliced
15 ml/1 tbls Worcestershire
    sauce
salt and pepper
a pinch of grated nutmeg
750 g/1½ lb cooked peeled
    prawns
15 ml/1 tbls chopped parsley

Serves 6

Soak the bread and bay leaf in the milk for 30 minutes. Remove the bay leaf and mash the bread. Beat the butter, eggs, green pepper, onions and sauce and season with salt, pepper and nutmeg. Stir in the prawns and parsley.

    Pour the mixture into a greased ovenproof dish and bake, uncovered, in the oven at 190C/375F/gas 5 for 35-40 minutes, until the top is crisp and golden brown. Serve at once.

    A cool green salad is the perfect partner.

OYSTER FRITTERS

Here is a recipe that's perfection with fresh oysters, and very tasty with canned or bottled ones. In the American South, the fritters are served with deep-fried corn cakes known as Hush puppies (page 158).

12 large oysters*, shelled, or
    500g/1lb canned or bottled
    oysters, drained, rinsed,
    and chopped
4 large eggs, separated
30 ml/2 tbls single cream
salt and pepper
50 g/2 oz flour
butter, for shallow frying
1 lemon, quartered

Serves 4

Beat the cream and egg yolks with salt, pepper and flour until the mixture is creamy. Stir in the chopped oysters. Whisk the egg whites until stiff and fold into the oyster mixture. Brush a griddle iron or heavy-based frying pan with butter and, when it is hot, drop on 30 ml/2 tablespoons of the mixture. Fry over medium heat until the fritters are set and brown on the underside. Flip them over and fry on the other side. Keep them hot while you fry the remaining mixture. Serve very hot, with lemon wedges.

* You can use clams in place of the oysters for a very agreeable alternative.

OYSTERS ROCKEFELLER

Invented at Antoine's, one of New York's most prestigious restaurants, this is a dish whose very name spells luxury. Once you've opened the oysters, the meal is cooked in a matter of moments without any last-minute fuss.

24 large oysters, opened (they
    are served on the half shell)
125 g/4 oz rock salt
150 g/6 oz unsalted butter,
    softened
150 g/6 oz cooked spinach,
    very thoroughly drained
    and finely chopped
6 spring onions, finely
    chopped
1 celery heart, finely chopped
15 ml/1 tbls chopped chervil,
    if available
30 ml/2 tbls chopped parsley
15 ml/1 tbls chopped
    marjoram
salt and pepper
a pinch of cayenne pepper
45 ml/3 tbls anisette (e.g.
    Pernod) – optional
lemon wedges, to serve

Serves 6

Mix together the butter, spinach, onion, celery and herbs and season with salt, pepper, cayenne, and anisette if used. Beat the mixture until smooth, cover and chill for 10 minutes.

    Spread the rock salt evenly in a large shallow baking dish and carefully place the oysters in a single layer on top. Divide the filling mixture between the oysters, pressing it to cover the edges completely and thus enclose the brine.

    Bake in the oven at 240C/475F/gas 9 for 10 minutes, until the topping is turning brown. Lift the oysters from the salt layer and serve at once with lemon wedges and brown bread and butter.

MARYLAND CRAB CAKES

This is a perfect way to enjoy a taste of Maryland cooking, even if the crab meat comes packaged.

500 g/1 lb crab meat
60 ml/4 tbls vegetable oil
1 medium onion, grated
1 clove garlic, crushed
125 g/4 oz breadcrumbs
1 canned pimento, finely
   chopped
10 ml/2 tsp lemon juice
5 ml/1 tsp Worcestershire
   sauce
15 ml/1 tbls tarragon mustard
salt and pepper
3 eggs, separated
50 g/2 oz ground almonds
oil or butter, for shallow
   frying
2 lemons, quartered, to serve
parsley sprigs, to garnish

Serves 6

Heat a little of the oil, and fry the onion and garlic over moderate heat for 3 minutes, stirring once or twice . Stir this into the crab meat, add the breadcrumbs, pimento, lemon juice, sauce and mustard and season with salt and pepper. Lightly beat the egg yolks and beat them into the mixture. Stiffly whisk the egg whites and fold them in. Cover the mixture and chill in the refrigerator for 30 minutes.

Shape it into flat cakes and coat them with the ground almonds.

Heat oil or butter and fry a few crab cakes at a time until they are brown on both sides. Serve hot with lemon wedges and garnished with parsley.

CRAB SOUFFLÉ

Whether your crab comes almost to your door or from the local freezer center, it can be lifted into a highly impressive dish that makes a good starter or main course.

250 g/8 oz crab meat
25 g/1oz dry breadcrumbs
50 g/2oz butter
25 g/1oz flour
300 ml/½ pt single cream
25 g/1 oz grated cheese
30 ml/2 tbls medium sherry
salt and pepper
4 eggs, separated

Serves 4

Grease a 600 ml/1pt soufflé dish and line the base and sides with breadcrumbs. Melt the butter, stir in the flour and gradually pour on the cream, stirring all the time. Simmer very gently for 3 minutes. Stir in the crab meat, cheese and sherry, season with salt and pepper and remove from the heat. Beat in the egg yolks one at a time. Leave to cool.

Stiffly whisk the egg whites and fold them into the crab mixture. Turn into the prepared soufflé dish and level the top. Sprinkle it with a fine layer of crumbs. Bake in the oven at 190C/375F/gas 5 for 40 minutes, or until the soufflé is well risen and firm on the outside.

LOBSTER-POT RING MOLD

Photograph on page 6

A mold of fish and cheese cubes separated by shiny grains of American rice – it's a summer dish you could take anywhere.

175 g/6 oz long-grain rice
salt
125 g/4 oz frozen mixed corn
   kernels, peas and red
   pepper
90 ml/6 tbls French dressing
   (page 92)
175 g/6 oz can tuna, drained
   and flaked
4 spring onions, finely
   chopped
15 ml/1 tbls chopped parsley
125 g/4 oz cheese, such as
   Double Gloucester, finely
   diced
pepper
45 g/3 tbls mayonnaise
1 bunch radishes, thinly
   sliced
1 bunch watercress sprigs
a few prawns, to garnish
   (optional)

Serves 6

Cook the rice in boiling, salted water for 12 minutes, or until it is just tender. Drain, refresh it in cold water, and drain again thoroughly. Cook the frozen vegetables in boiling, salted water for 3 minutes, then drain. Toss the rice and vegetables in the French dressing and leave to cool.

Stir in the tuna, spring onions, parsley and cheese. Season with pepper and stir in the mayonnaise. Spoon the mixture into a lightly-oiled 1-liter/1¾-pt ring mold and press it down well. Chill in the refrigerator for about 3 hours.

Turn the mold out on to a flat serving plate and arrange a ring of radish slices around it. Fill the center with watercress and prawns, if available, to garnish.

3: MEAT AND POULTRY

Americans have always been what one might respectfully call "large meat-eaters." Recent statistics show that the "average American" consumes 80 kg/175 lb of beef, pork, veal and lamb and 20 kg/45 lb of poultry, apart from an unspecified amount of game birds, in every year – which adds up to some 30 percent of the world's meat consumption. Pork has a proud place in American history, though beef has long since overtaken it in the nation's affections. The early Settlers, fearful of finding a barren land, brought pigs from England and turned them loose to forage in the woods, fattening them at no cost to the farms and to some effect in terms of flavor. Indeed, this self-sought diet of protein and fiber is held to account for the now-famous flavor of Virginia hams, salted, spiced and hung to smoke over oak, apple and hickory chips.

Pickling and smoking meats were vital accomplishments to ensure survival in the harsh winters, and not a morsel was wasted. Slices of salt pork would be crispy-fried with quartered apples; pork cubes would find their way into dishes as different as clam chowder, baked beans and braised cabbage, and bacon was a staple food to be eked out with muffins, hominy grits, johnny cake, corn bread, pancakes, flapjacks, fried potatoes or greens. In the Deep South, hams were thickly sliced and fried to make the kind of breakfast you could really go to work on – as long as you liked it served with coffee gravy, that is!

Pork scraps were mixed with other meats and made into tasty supper or journey pies; spiced, flavored and squeezed into sausage casings; or blended with other meats in hamburgers, meat balls and meat loaves. All these recipes, good as they were, have survived and are still family favorites.

Some of the earliest recipes enlightening American housewives on the mysteries of cooking beef tell a tale about its quality. One goes so far as to recommend drilling some

5-7.5 cm/2-3 in into the meat to insert strips of salt pork for larding, and others describe that well-known tenderizing trick, marinating in oil and vinegar or wine with herbs and spices.

The quality of American beef has come a very long way since the days when it consisted of work-weary oxen or beef cattle that might have been driven a thousand miles to market, and no doubt accounts for the fact that the housewife chooses beef in favor of other meats on four out of every seven occasions and then prefers to broil or roast it.

Modern communications have robbed us all of our culinary secrets and given so many regional dishes international fame and status. The Mexican cuisine which crossed the border and settled on the Texans like a well-fitting cape is a prime example, giving rise to the affectionate Tex-Mex label. Spiced tomato and chilli sauce with meat loaves and paté, chilli con carne, and enchiladas, have made our culinary repertoire all the richer. Chicken, though not the Sunday-best treat it once was, has retained its popularity by virtue of its versatility – chicken in tortillas, pancakes, with pasta, in burgers, filled with bacon and walnuts and roasted to a honey glow – it can never be dull.

Duck is a comparative newcomer to the US, having made the journey by Clipper from China to New York only in 1873. It is the perfect foil for a fund of fruit sauces and accompaniments, among them grapefruits, oranges, cherries and peaches.

Wild game and birds abounded in early America, although there are now said to be even more wild deer than there were in pioneering days. Rabbits, pheasants (confusingly also called ruffed grouse and partridge), wild duck, quail, squab – if only there were a whole book, and not just a single chapter, we could do justice to the wealth of ways to cook them.

CASSEROLED PHEASANT WITH CHESTNUTS

This delicious way to cook not-so-young game birds still has a hint of the old pioneering days.

2 pheasants
50 g/2 oz butter
350 g/12 oz shallots or button onions
250 g/8 oz canned whole chestnuts, drained
15 ml/1 tbls flour
450 ml/¾ pt brown stock (page 12), hot
grated rind and juice of ½ orange
10 ml/2 tsp redcurrant jelly
salt and pepper
30 ml/2 tbls double cream

Serves 6-8

Melt the butter in a flameproof dish and cook the birds to brown them evenly on all sides. Remove the pheasants and keep them warm. Fry the onions and chestnuts in the fat for 4 minutes over moderate heat, stirring once or twice, and remove them. Stir in the flour, then gradually pour on the hot stock, stirring until it simmers. Stir in the orange rind and juice and the jelly and season with salt and pepper.

Return the pheasants, onions and chestnuts to the dish and cover. Cook in the oven at 180C/350F/gas 4 for 1 hour.

Arrange the birds on a heated serving dish and spoon the onions and chestnuts around them. Bring the sauce to the boil and fast-boil for 5 minutes. Stir in the cream and adjust the seasoning. Pour a little over the birds to garnish, and serve the rest separately.

RABBIT WITH PRUNES

A variation on a dish from Wyoming. The meat is marinated overnight to ensure that it is moist and tender.

1 young rabbit, jointed
250 g/8 oz stoned prunes
300 ml/½ pt unsweetened orange juice
30 ml/2 tbls vegetable oil
40 g/1½ oz butter
15 g/½ oz flour
300 ml/½ pt brown stock (page 12), hot
150 ml/¼ pt red wine
salt and pepper
Marinade
60 ml/4 tbls vegetable oil
45 ml/3 tbls red wine vinegar
grated rind and juice of 1 orange
1 bay leaf
1 small onion, sliced
6 black peppercorns, crushed
a few parsley stalks

Serves 4

Mix together the marinade ingredients and pour over the rabbit. Cover and leave to soak for at least 8 hours, turning the rabbit at intervals. Soak the prunes in the orange juice. Lift out the rabbit pieces and dry them.

Melt the oil and butter in a flameproof casserole and, over moderate heat, brown the rabbit pieces evenly on all sides. Remove the rabbit and stir in the flour. Gradually pour on the stock and wine, stirring. Bring the sauce to the boil and simmer for 2 minutes. Add the prunes and any remaining orange juice and season with salt and pepper.

Cover the dish and cook in the oven at 180C/350F/gas 4 for 2 hours. Lift out the rabbit and prunes. Boil the sauce over high heat to thicken it, adjust the seasoning and return the meat and prunes to the dish. Serve with boiled potatoes.

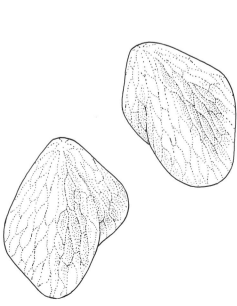

ROAST DUCK WITH STUFFED APPLES

1 duck, about 2.25 kg/5 lb
salt
25 g/1 oz butter
1 small onion, finely chopped
1 celery stalk, finely chopped
the duck's liver, chopped
4 dessert apples
25 g/1 oz breadcrumbs
30 ml/2 tbls hazelnuts, finely
    chopped
grated rind and juice of 1
    orange
pepper

Serves 4-5

Prick the duck well all over and rub the skin with salt.
Place it on a rack in the roasting pan and cook at 180C/350F/gas
4 for about 2½ hours. (Calculate the cooking time at 35
minutes per 500 g/1 lb.)

  Meanwhile, prepare the apples. Melt the butter and fry the
onion, celery and duck liver over moderate heat for 3 minutes,
stirring once or twice. Cut a slice from the top of each apple
and scoop out the core and some of the flesh, taking care to
leave firm "walls". Chop the apple flesh and mix with the
breadcrumbs, nuts, orange rind and juice. Stir the nut mixture
into the pan with the celery mixture, season with salt and
pepper and mix well. Pack the stuffing into the apples. Score a
slit all around the center of each apple to prevent the skin from
bursting. Cook the apples with the duck for the last 20 minutes
of the cooking time. Serve with Cranberry sauce (page 71).

BABY CHICKENS WITH WALNUT STUFFING

A recipe from Carolina. The cream added to the sauce at the
last minute works wonders.

4 baby chickens (poussins)
vegetable oil, for brushing
10 ml/2 tsp flour
300 ml/½ pt chicken stock
    (page 12)
30 ml/2 tbls sherry
150 ml/½ pt double cream
Stuffing
120 ml/8 tbls cooked rice
75 g/3 oz chopped walnuts
grated rind and juice of 1
    orange
15 ml/1 tbls chopped parsley
30 ml/2 tbls melted butter
a pinch of sugar
salt and pepper

Serves 4

Wash and dry the chickens. Mix together the stuffing
ingredients and divide between the chickens. Tie the legs
with twine. Brush the birds with oil, season with salt and
pepper and place on a rack in a roasting pan.

  Roast at 200C/400F/gas 6 for 40 minutes, or until the birds
are cooked. To check, pierce the thickest part of the leg with a
fine skewer. The juices should run clear.

  Transfer the chickens to a heated serving dish. Strain most
of the fat from the pan, stir in the flour and pour on the stock.
Bring to the boil, stirring, and simmer for 3 minutes.
Stir in the sherry and cream and season with salt and pepper.
Heat the sauce without boiling.

  Pour a little sauce over the chickens to garnish and serve the
rest separately.

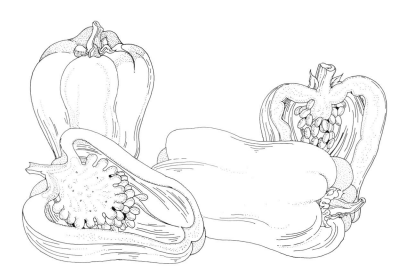

CHICKEN LASAGNE

Photograph on page 44

175 g/6 oz "no pre-cook"
   green lasagne
75 g/3 oz butter
1 medium onion, finely
   chopped
40 g/1½ oz flour
300 ml/½ pt chicken stock
   (page 12), hot
300 ml/½ pt milk
salt and pepper
a pinch of grated nutmeg
175 g/6 oz cooked bacon,
   finely chopped
250 g/8 oz cooked chicken,
   finely chopped
125 g/4 oz button
   mushrooms, sliced
15 ml/1 tbls lemon juice
300 ml/½ pt soured cream
1 egg
75 g/3 oz grated Parmesan
   cheese

Serves 4

Melt half the butter and fry the onion over moderate heat for
3 minutes, stirring occasionally. Stir in the flour and cook for
1 minute. Gradually pour on the stock and the milk and bring
to the boil, stirring all the time until the sauce has thickened.
Season with salt, pepper and nutmeg and stir in the bacon and
chicken. Cook the mushrooms in the remaining butter with
the lemon juice. Season well with pepper.

   Spoon a layer of the chicken sauce into a greased ovenproof
dish, cover with a layer of lasagne, then more sauce, the
mushrooms and another layer of lasagne. Beat together the
soured cream and egg and spread over the lasagne. Top with
the grated cheese.

   Bake in the oven at 190C/375F/gas 5 for 35 minutes, or until
the top is bubbling and golden. Serve hot.

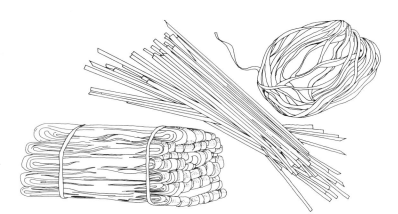

CHICKEN AND HAMBURGER

Photograph on page 36

It's getting into troubled waters to speculate where
hamburgers originated and just what the magic ingredients
were! This recipe comes from Connecticut.

500 g/1 lb unsmoked gammon
500 g/1 lb raw chicken
10 ml/2 tsp French mustard
5 ml/1 tsp Worcestershire
   sauce
salt and pepper
8 baps, toasted and split
shredded lettuce, to serve
oil, for brushing

Makes 8

Finely mince the meats together. Mash them with a wooden
spoon until they begin to bind together, then beat in the
mustard and sauce. Season with salt and pepper.

   Shape the meat into 8 round flat cakes. Brush them with oil
and cook under a hot grill for about 12 minutes on each side,
until they are crisp on the outside but still moist inside.

   Serve them in the toasted and split baps, garnished with the
lettuce and with a selection of sauces and chutneys.

   For a more substantial meal, serve the burgers on rounds of
toast, with grilled tomatoes and mushrooms.

CHICKEN SCALLOPS

Photograph opposite

The presentation, in scallop shells or shallow dishes, makes
this dish as visually appealing as it is appetizing.

175 g/6 oz short-cut macaroni
salt
45 ml/3 tbls vegetable oil
1 large onion, chopped
4 rashers streaky bacon, rind
   removed, chopped
175 g/6 oz button mushrooms
175 g/6 oz cooked chicken,
   chopped
pepper
200 ml/7 fl oz double cream
60 ml/4 tbls breadcrumbs
75 g/3 oz grated cheese
parsley sprigs, to garnish

Serves 4

Cook the macaroni in boiling, salted water with 15 ml/1 tbls of
the oil for 10 minutes, or until it is just tender. Drain, refresh it
in warm water and drain again.

   Heat the remaining oil and fry the onion over moderate heat
for 2 minutes. Add the bacon, stir and cook for 2 minutes, then
add the mushrooms and cook for a further 2 minutes. Stir in
the chicken and macaroni, season with pepper and heat
through. Add the cream, stir well and heat gently.

   Divide the mixture between 4 greased ovenproof dishes
and sprinkle the breadcrumbs and then the cheese on top.
Brown under a medium grill for 3-4 minutes. Garnish with the
parsley and serve at once.

TEX-MEX CHILLI CON CARNE

There are countless variations of this world-famous dish. Some include the red kidney beans, as our recipe does, and others - which claim greater authenticity – do not.

250 g/8 oz dried red kidney
    beans, soaked overnight
    and drained
1 kg/2½ lb lean braising
    steak, trimmed of excess fat
    and cut into 2.5-cm/1-in
    cubes
60 ml/4 tbls vegetable oil
1 large onion, finely chopped
2 cloves garlic, finely chopped
2.5-5 ml/½-1 tsp chilli
    powder, or according to
    taste
450 ml/¾ pt brown stock
    (page 12)
150 ml/¼ pt red wine
15 ml/1 tbls flour
salt
a few parsley stalks
2 bay leaves
10 ml/2 tsp dried oregano

Serves 6-8

Put the beans in a pan, well-cover them with cold water, bring them to the boil and boil rapidly for 15 minutes. Cover the pan and simmer for 45 minutes. Drain the beans.

Meanwhile, heat the oil in a flameproof casserole and fry the meat, a few pieces at a time, over moderately high heat for about 5 minutes. Stir the meat frequently so that it browns evenly. Remove the meat and keep it warm.

Add the onion and garlic and fry it over moderate heat for 3 minutes, stirring frequently. Stir in the chilli powder. Return the meat to the pan, pour on the stock and wine, season with salt and add the parsley, bay leaves and oregano. Bring to the boil, cover the dish and simmer for 1 hour.

Stir a little of the hot stock into the flour to make a smooth paste, add more stock, stirring, and pour over the meat. Stir over moderate heat until the sauce is smooth. Add the partly-cooked beans, taste the sauce and adjust the seasoning. Cover the dish, return to the boil and simmer over low heat for 45 minutes – 1 hour, or until the meat is tender. Discard the bay leaves and parsley. Serve with rice.

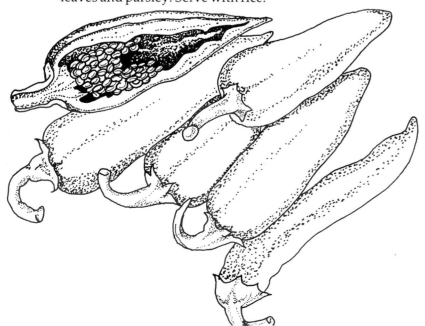

CHEESEBURGERS

No over-the-counter burgers can ever compete with the ones you can make – so quickly and easily – at home.

500 g/1 lb topside of beef, cut
    into cubes
1 medium onion, quartered
10 ml/2 tsp French mustard
15 ml/1 tbls Worcestershire
    sauce
1.5 ml/¼ tsp ground mace
salt and pepper
oil, for brushing
4 thin slices Gruyère cheese
4 baps, toasted

Makes 4

Finely mince the beef and onion. Beat in the mustard, sauce and mace and season with salt and pepper. Shape into 4 round flat cakes. Brush them with oil and cook under a hot grill for about 2 minutes on each side. Cover each burger with a cheese slice and grill until it is bubbling.

Serve the cheeseburgers in a toasted bap, with Spiced tomato sauce (page 170).

SWEET AND SOUR RIBS

Spare ribs of pork, popularized by the take-away Chinese restaurants, are easily cooked at home. Serve them with rice or noodles and a stir-fried green vegetable.

1 kg/2¼ lb pork spare ribs,
    separated
60 ml/4 tbls red wine vinegar
75 ml/5 tbls tomato purée
30 ml/2 tbls soy sauce
45 ml/3 tbls clear honey
15 ml/1 tbls vegetable oil
300 ml/½ pt brown stock
    (page 12)
salt

Serves 4

Arrange the ribs in a single layer in a shallow ovenproof dish. Mix together all the remaining ingredients and pour over the meat. Baste the meat, cover and leave at room temperature for 2-3 hours, turning it in the sauce occasionally.

Bake the ribs in the oven at 200C/400F/gas 6, basting them frequently, for 45 minutes. Lower the heat to 180C/350F/gas 4 and cook for a further 1 hour, basting frequently and uncovering the dish for the last 20 minutes. Serve hot.

BRAISED VENISON

Venison is not the survival means it once was, but it makes an exciting dish with the flavor of the wild. Marinating is advisable to tenderize and flavor the meat.

1.5-kg/3½-lb haunch of
  venison
30 ml/2 tbls vegetable oil
40 g/1½ oz butter
2 medium onions, thinly
  sliced
3 medium carrots, thinly
  sliced
4 celery stalks, thinly sliced
2 bay leaves
a few parsley stalks
450 ml/¾ pt brown stock
  (page 12)
salt and pepper
30 ml/2 tbls redcurrant jelly
15 ml/1 tbls flour
Marinade
150 ml/¼ pt red wine
60 ml/4 tbls vegetable oil
1 small onion, chopped
2 bay leaves
6 juniper berries, crushed
4 allspice berries, crushed

Serves 6-8

Trim the meat and place it in a dish. Mix together all the marinade ingredients and pour it over the meat. Cover and leave for 24 hours, turning the meat occasionally. Lift the meat from the marinade and dry it.

Melt the oil and 25 g/1 oz of the butter in a large flameproof casserole and fry the onions, carrots and celery over medium heat for 5 minutes, stirring frequently. Remove the vegetables and fry the meat on all sides until it is evenly brown. Return the vegetables to the pan, add the bay leaves and the parsley, pour on the stock and season with salt and pepper.

Bring to the boil, cover the pan and cook in the oven at 180C/350F/gas 4, turning the meat occasionally, for 3 hours or until the meat is tender..

Transfer the meat to a heated serving dish, arrange the vegetables around it and keep them warm. Skim the fat from the top of the stock and remove the bay leaves and parsley. Stir in the redcurrant jelly. Simmer for 3 minutes. Beat together the remaining butter and the flour and stir into the sauce a little at a time. Taste and adjust the seasoning. Bring the sauce to the boil, stirring, and simmer for 3 minutes. Serve separately.

STIR-FRIED BEEF AND CAULIFLOWER

Photograph on page 45

A Westernized dish in the "fast-food" category.

500 g/1 lb top rump beef,
  trimmed and cut into
  6-mm/¼-in strips
450 ml/¾ pt brown stock
  (page 12)
30 ml/2 tbls soy sauce
1 small cauliflower, cut into
  florets
75 ml/5 tbls vegetable oil
1 large onion, thinly sliced
2 thin celery stalks, thinly
  sliced
1 clove garlic, chopped
30 ml/2 tbls flour
salt and pepper
45 ml/3 tbls dry sherry

Serves 4

Heat the stock with 15 ml/1 tbls soy sauce, add the cauliflower florets and boil for 3 minutes. Lift out the cauliflower and reserve the stock. Heat the oil in a frying-pan or wok and fry the onion, celery and garlic over high heat, stirring constantly for 1 minute. Toss the meat in the flour seasoned with salt and pepper, add to the pan and stir-fry for 2 minutes. Add the cauliflower, reserved stock, remaining soy sauce and sherry, bring to the boil and simmer over moderate heat for 2 minutes, stirring occasionally. Serve over rice.

CORNED BEEF HASH

Some people make it with left-over mashed potatoes, others prefer it this way, with rice. Either way, it's amazingly good.

350 g/12 oz cooked long-grain
  rice
350 g/12 oz corned beef,
  chopped
1 small onion, finely chopped
salt and pepper
2 eggs, beaten
50 g/2 oz butter

Serves 4

Mix together the rice, corned beef and onion, season with salt and pepper and beat in the eggs.

Melt half the butter in a frying-pan, add the corned beef mixture and press it down evenly. Fry over moderately high heat until the base is well browned and has formed a crust. Place a large plate over the pan and quickly invert. Melt the remaining butter in the pan, slide the hash back and cook until the underside is brown and well crusted.

Serve hot, with chutney and mustard.

NEW ENGLAND BOILED DINNER

This dish was originally made with home-cured beef, a one-pot meal that involved no work on the Sabbath. The thrifty Puritans turned left-over meat into Red Flannel hash (page 147 in "Snacks" section).

2 kg/4½ lb salt silverside of
    beef
500 g/1 lb small potatoes
    (halved if necessary)
500 g/1 lb carrots, thickly
    sliced
1 small swede, diced
pepper
1 small firm head of cabbage,
    cut into 8 wedges
250 g/8 oz shallots

Serves 8

Put the beef into a large flameproof casserole, cover with water and bring to the boil. Skim off the foam, cover the pan and simmer for 3 hours, topping up with more boiling water so that the meat is covered.

Add the potatoes, carrots and swede and season with pepper. Return to the boil, cover and simmer for 15 minutes. Add the cabbage and shallots, bring back to the boil, cover and simmer for a further 15 minutes.

Transfer the meat to a heated serving dish and surround it with the vegetables. Skim the fat from the stock and serve it separately.

STEAK TARTARE

Raw steak is not to everyone's taste, but there is something so basic – so "back-to-nature" – about it that it merits a place.

500 g/1 lb finest fillet of beef,
    finely minced 3 times,
    chilled
2 egg yolks
75 ml/5 tbls olive oil
30 ml/2 tbls German mustard
10 ml/2 tsp tomato purée
salt and pepper
10 ml/2 tsp Tabasco sauce
5 ml/1 tsp soy sauce
2 cloves garlic, crushed
1 small onion, finely chopped
2 dill cucumbers, finely
    chopped
30 ml/2 tbls capers, chopped
4 anchovy fillets, finely
    chopped
lettuce leaves, to serve
parsley sprigs, to garnish

Serves 2

Pound the steak in a bowl and beat in the egg yolks. When they have been absorbed, gradually beat in the oil, then the mustard and tomato purée. Season with salt and pepper and beat in the sauces, garlic, onion, cucumber and capers. Beat until the mixture is well blended.

Line a serving dish with lettuce leaves, pile on the steak mixture and garnish with parsley. Serve well chilled.

HUNGARIAN VEAL WITH PAPRIKA SAUCE

One of the many dishes that traveled to America in the repertoire of Eastern European immigrants. It now fits perfectly into the "fast food" mold.

6 veal escalopes
50 g/2 oz butter
1 medium onion, finely
    chopped
2 cloves garlic, crushed
10 ml/2 tsp paprika
10 ml/2 tsp flour
100 ml/3½ fl oz red vermouth
salt and pepper
150 ml/¼ pt soured cream
15 ml/1 tbls chopped parsley,
    to garnish

Serves 6

Melt the butter in a large frying-pan and fry the veal for 2 minutes each side over high heat. Lower the heat and cook the veal for 4-5 minutes on each side. Remove the meat and keep it warm.

Fry the onion and garlic over moderate heat for 3 minutes, stir in the paprika and then the flour and stir for 1 minute. Pour on the vermouth, stirring, season with salt and pepper and simmer for 2-3 minutes. Add the soured cream. Allow the sauce just to heat through. Pour over the meat and sprinkle with the parsley. Serve with rice.

GRILLED STEAK FINGERS

1 kg/2¼ lb sirloin steak
3 spring onions, chopped
4 cloves garlic, crushed
75 ml/5 tbls soy sauce
30 ml/2 tbls sesame oil
50 g/2 oz soft light brown
    sugar
30 ml/2 tbls medium sherry
60 ml/4 tbls red wine
pepper

Serves 6

Cut the steak across the grain into thin finger-sized pieces.

Mix together the onions and garlic, stir in the soy sauce, oil and sugar, sherry and wine and season with pepper. Put the steak into a shallow dish, pour over the marinade, cover and leave to marinate at room temperature for at least 2 hours, or overnight if more convenient.

Remove the steak from the marinade, reserving the liquid. Cook the steak under a moderately high grill for 6-9 minutes, turning frequently and brushing with the marinade. Heat the remaining marinade and serve it separately as a sauce. Serve with noodles.

CHATEAUBRIAND STEAK WITH BRANDY SAUCE

Chateaubriand steak is a double fillet, beaten into a large round and cut across the grain for pan-frying or broiling.

1 kg/2¼ lb Chateaubriand
   steak
45-60 ml/3-4 tbls vegetable oil
salt and pepper
10 ml/2 tsp mustard powder
25g/1 oz butter
10 ml/2 tsp flour
15 ml/1 tbls lemon juice
45 ml/3 tbls Worcestershire
   sauce
150 ml/¼ pt brandy
30 ml/2 tbls double cream
parsley sprigs, to garnish

Serves 4 – 6

Beat the meat with a wet rolling-pin and tie it firmly into a neat circle. Heat 45 ml/3 tbls oil in a heavy-based frying-pan over high heat. When it is smoking hot, sear the meat for 2 minutes, first on one side and then the other. Lower the heat to moderate. Mix together the salt, pepper and mustard and rub it into the meat and cook for a further 3-4 minutes on each side, or according to how rare you like it. Add more oil if necessary.

Remove the meat from the pan and keep warm. Add the butter and, when it melts, stir in the flour. Add the lemon juice, sauce and brandy and bring to simmering point, stirring. Stir in the cream and adjust seasoning. Do not allow the sauce to boil.

Pour a little of the sauce over the steak and serve the rest separately. Carve the steak in very thin slices.

SUPPER PLAIT

250 g/8 oz frozen puff pastry,
 thawed
250 g/8 oz pork sausagemeat
1 small onion, finely chopped
a pinch of grated nutmeg
1.5 ml/¼ tsp ground allspice
5 ml/1 tsp chopped parsley
5 ml/1 tsp chopped chives
salt and pepper
4 hard-boiled eggs, chopped
1 egg, beaten

Serves 4

Roll out the pastry on a lightly-floured board to an oblong 30 ×
25 cm/12×10 in. Transfer the pastry to a greased baking sheet.
Break up the sausagemeat and beat in the onion, herbs and
spices and season with salt and pepper. Stir in the chopped
eggs. Shape the filling into a roll and place it along the center of
the pastry.
 Cut through the pastry on each side, making diagonal
slashes 1 cm/½ in wide. Brush the pastry with half the beaten
egg.
 Wrap the pastry strips over to enclose the filling, alternately
from each side, to resemble a plait and trim the ends. Brush the
pastry top with the remaining egg. Bake in the oven at 200C/
400F/gas 6 for 35 minutes, or until the top is golden brown.
Serve hot, with Spiced tomato sauce (page 170) or cold with
herb mayonnaise.

HOMESTEAD PATÉ

1 kg/2¼ lb belly of pork
250 g/8 oz pig's liver
1 medium onion
1 egg, lightly beaten
5 ml/1 tsp salt
5 ml/1 tsp pepper
2.5 ml/½ tsp ground allspice
15 ml/1 tbls chive mustard
15 ml/1 tbls chopped parsley
15 ml/1 tbls flour
8 bacon rashers, rind
    removed
shredded lettuce, to serve
radishes and parsley, to
    garnish

Serves 8

Cut the rind and any bones from the pork. Mince it finely with
the liver and onion. Beat in the egg, salt, pepper, allspice,
mustard, parsley and flour.

Line a 900-ml/2-lb loaf tin with the bacon rashers and spoon
in the meat mixture. Press it level to the top and cover with
foil.

Stand the loaf tin in a roasting tin containing 2.5 cm/1in cold
water. Cook in the oven at 190C/375F/gas 5 for 1½ hours.

Cool the paté in the tin. Turn it out on to a dish lined with
shredded lettuce. Garnish with sliced radishes and parsley
sprigs.

MEAT LOAF

Photograph opposite

A simple loaf of ground beef which can be as pepped-up as
you like, depending on the sauce you choose.

500 g/1 lb lean topside of beef
250 g/8 oz lean pork, e.g. leg
250 g/8 oz pig's kidney
1 small onion
60 ml/4 tbls bread cubes
15 ml/1 tbls chopped
    rosemary
2 cloves garlic, crushed
5 ml/1 tsp ground allspice
salt and pepper
1 egg, lightly beaten
parsley sprigs and tomato, to
    garnish

Serves 6-8

Mince the beef, pork, kidney, onion and bread. If you use a
food processor, chop the meats finely but do not grind them to
a paste. Stir in the rosemary, garlic and spice and season well
with salt and pepper. Bind the mixture with the egg.

Turn the mixture into a greased 900-ml/2-lb loaf tin and
press it well down. Cover with foil, stand the tin on a baking
tray and bake in the oven at 180C/350F/gas 4 for 1 hour.
Remove the foil and continue cooking for 15 minutes. Serve
hot, on a bed of rice, with Chilli sauce (page 170) or Spiced
tomato sauce (page 170).

The loaf is also good served cold.

BEEF POT ROAST

Photograph opposite

A large dish of tender, pot-roasted beef casts a backward glance at the chuck-wagon era.

1.5 kg/3¼ lb silverside of beef
45 ml/3 tbls vegetable oil
2 celery stalks, thinly sliced
6 shallots, peeled
15 ml/1 tbls flour
peas and carrots, to serve
Marinade
300 ml/½ pt red wine
45 ml/3 tbls vegetable oil
salt and pepper
1.5 ml/¼ tsp paprika
2 cloves garlic, crushed
2 bay leaves
4 juniper berries, crushed

Serves 6

Put the beef in a deep casserole. Mix together the marinade ingredients and pour them over the meat. Set aside for 8 hours, turning the meat if possible. Lift out the meat, reserving the marinade.

Heat the oil in a flameproof casserole and brown the meat on all sides. Stir in the celery and shallots and cook for 1 minute. Pour on the marinade and cover the casserole. Cook in the oven at 170C/325F/gas 2 for 2 hours. Remove the lid, baste the meat and cook, uncovered, for 30 minutes, or until the meat is tender.

Transfer the meat to a heated serving dish. Strain the juices, stir a little into the flour to make a smooth paste, then stir them together. Bring to the boil, adjust seasoning and serve the sauce separately. Arrange the vegetables around the meat.

BEEF GOULASH

Photograph opposite

This Hungarian combination of beef, spices and soured cream has proved very much to American tastes.

50 g/2 oz beef dripping
750 g/1 ½ lb chuck steak,
    trimmed and cut into
    2.5-cm/1-in cubes
2 medium onions, sliced
2 cloves garlic, crushed
15 ml/1 tbls paprika
2.5 ml/½ tsp cayenne pepper
15 ml/1 tbls flour
600 ml/1 pt brown stock (page
    12), hot
30 ml/2 tbls tomato purée
salt and pepper
150 ml/¼ pt soured cream, or
    plain yoghurt

Serves 4

Heat the dripping and brown the meat on all sides. Remove the meat and add the onions, garlic, paprika and cayenne. Stir well and fry for 1-2 minutes. Stir in the flour and fry for 1 further minute. Return the meat to the pan and pour on the hot stock, stirring all the time. Stir in the tomato purée and season with salt and pepper.

Cover the dish and simmer for 2 hours. Stir in half of the soured cream or yoghurt and swirl the rest on top.

LIVER WITH AVOCADOS

Have everything ready and you can cook this dish before guests realise you're missing. The pinky-red liver and creamy-green avocados are a fabulous combination.

500 g/1 lb calf's liver, cut into
    6-mm/¼-in thick slices
60 ml/4 tbls flour
salt and pepper
a pinch of ground mace
15 ml/1 tbls olive oil
50 g/2 oz butter
12 fresh sage leaves
2 avocados
45 ml/3 tbls orange juice
90 ml/6 tbls chicken stock
    (page 12)
45 ml/3 tbls Marsala

Serves 4

Season the flour with salt, pepper and mace and toss the liver to coat the slices on both sides. Melt the oil and butter in a frying-pan, add the sage leaves and fry the liver slices over moderately high heat for 1 minute on each side. Transfer the liver to a serving dish and keep it warm.

Halve, stone, peel and slice the avocados and brush them with orange juice. Stir the remaining orange juice, chicken stock and Marsala into the pan. Stir well, bring to the boil and season the sauce with salt and pepper. Pour the sauce over the liver and arrange the avocado slices on top. Serve with creamed potatoes.

LIVER CRUMBLE

Photograph opposite

A true farmhouse dish that makes not-so-glamorous ingredients into something tasty.

500 g/1 lb lamb's liver
6 rashers back bacon
2 small leeks, thinly sliced
45 ml/3 tbls vegetable oil
45 ml/3 tbls chopped parsley
150 ml/¼ pt chicken stock
   (page 12)
salt and pepper
Topping
75 g/3 oz flour
10 ml/2 tsp mustard powder
50 g/2 oz butter
25 g/1 oz strong Cheddar
   cheese, grated
25 g/1 oz porridge oats

Serves 4

Trim the liver and cut it into thin slices. Cut the rind from the bacon and cut into 2-cm/¾-in squares. Heat 30 ml/2 tbls oil and fry the liver slices for 1 minute on each side. Remove from the pan and fry the bacon for 2 minutes, stirring once or twice. Add the remaining oil and fry the leeks for 3-4 minutes, stirring frequently. Layer the liver, bacon and leeks in a casserole, seasoning well between each layer with salt, pepper and parsley. Pour on the stock.

To make the topping, mix together the flour and mustard and season with salt and pepper. Rub in the butter and stir in the cheese and oats. Sprinkle over the casserole.

Bake in the oven at 200C/400F/gas 6 for 35 minutes, until the topping is crisp and golden brown. If necessary, put it under a hot grill for a couple of minutes.

Serve with mashed potatoes and green vegetables.

58

SPICED LAMB MEATBALLS

Photograph opposite

500 g/1 lb lean leg of lamb,
   finely minced
1 small onion, finely chopped
1 egg, lightly beaten
15 ml/1 tbls seedless raisins
30 ml/2 tbls chopped walnuts
30 ml/2 tbls chopped parsley
5 ml/1 tsp ground allspice
2.5 ml/½ tsp ground
   cinnamon
salt and pepper
oil, for shallow frying

Serves 6

Beat the minced meat with a wooden spoon to form a paste.
Beat in all the remaining ingredients and knead until smooth.
Flour your hands and shape the mixture into rounds about the
size of golf balls.
   Heat the oil and fry the meatballs a few at a time, turning
them frequently, until they are crisp and deep brown on the
outside. Toss them on kitchen paper to dry. Serve hot or cold.

LAMB AND GRAPEFRUIT ROLL

An economical family dish in which the richness of the meat is
balanced by the sunshine fruit.

2 × 750 g/1½ lb breasts of
   lamb
3 grapefruit
50 g/2 oz butter
1 large onion, finely chopped
1 clove garlic, crushed
125 g/4 oz breadcrumbs
30 ml/2 tbls chopped mint
15 ml/1 tbls chopped parsley
50 g/2 oz blanched slivered
   almonds
1 egg, lightly beaten
salt and pepper
1 bunch watercress sprigs, to
   garnish

Serves 6

Grate the rind of 1 grapefruit. Thinly pare the rind of another
and cut it into very thin strips. Simmer the strips for 15
minutes, drain, dry and set aside for the garnish. Segment all 3
grapefruits. Chop the segments of 2 of them and reserve the
other to garnish.
   Melt the butter and fry the onion and garlic over moderate
heat for 3 minutes, stirring once or twice. Remove from the
heat and stir in the breadcrumbs, the chopped grapefruit,
mint, parsley and almonds. Stir in the egg, season with salt
and pepper and mix well.
   Place one breast of lamb skin-side down, cover with the
stuffing and top with the other piece of lamb, skin-side up. Tie
at 5-cm/2-in intervals with string.
   Transfer the lamb to a baking dish and bake in the oven at
180C/350F/gas 4 for 1 hour. Increase the heat to 200C/400F/gas
6 and continue cooking for 20 minutes, to crisp the skin.
Remove the string and serve at once. Garnish the lamb with
the grapefruit strips and arrange the watercress and fruit
segments around it.

BULGAR MEATBALLS

Americans have taken to using bulgar, or cracked wheat, as a
healthy meat-extender in burgers, meat loaves, paté and
casseroles. From North Dakota, here's a tasty way with meatballs.

125 g/4 oz bulgar
500 g/1 lb finely-minced rump
   steak
1 small onion, finely chopped
½ celery heart, finely chopped
5 ml/1 tsp dried oregano
grated rind of 1 lemon
salt and pepper
2 egg yolks, lightly beaten
30 ml/2 tbls vegetable oil
25 g/1 oz butter
Sauce
30 ml/2 tbls vegetable oil
1 medium onion, peeled and
   finely chopped
1 clove garlic, crushed
450 g/15 oz can tomatoes
30 ml/2 tbls tomato purée
2 canned pimentos, finely
   chopped
15 ml/1 tbls Worcestershire
   sauce
5 ml/1 tsp dried oregano
15 ml/1 tbls chopped parsley

Serves 6

Soak the bulgar in 125 ml/4 fl oz water for at least 1 hour.
   Mash the minced steak with a wooden spoon until it is soft
and moist. Stir in the bulgar, onion, celery, oregano and lemon
rind and season with salt and pepper. Beat in the egg yolks
and beat well until the mixture is fully blended. Flour your
hands and shape the mixture into 20 balls.
   Melt the oil and butter in a frying-pan and, when it is hot,
fry the meatballs over moderately high heat, turning them to
brown evenly on all sides. Remove them and keep them warm.
   Add the oil to the pan and fry the onion and garlic over
moderate heat for 3 minutes, stirring once or twice. Add the
tomatoes, tomato purée, pimentos, sauce and herbs and
season with salt and pepper. Stir well, bring to the boil and
simmer for 3 minutes. Return the meatballs to the pan, cover
and simmer over low heat for 30 minutes, turning the meat in
the sauce occasionally. Taste the sauce and adjust the
seasoning if necessary. Serve with rice.

BOSTON BAKED BEANS

Photograph opposite

This dish, which reheats particularly well, used to be made in New England on a Saturday, to be served without incurring further work on the Sabbath.

500 g/1 lb dried white haricot
   (navy) beans, soaked
   overnight and drained
45 ml/3 tbls molasses
15 ml/1 tbls soft dark brown
   sugar
5 ml/1 tsp mustard powder
600 ml/1 pt chicken stock
   (page 12), hot
1 medium onion
1 bacon knuckle
salt and pepper

Serves 6

Boil the beans in unsalted water for 1 hour, or until they are tender. Drain.
   Mix the molasses, sugar and mustard powder and gradually add the hot stock. Put the beans, onion and knuckle into a casserole, pour on the stock and add boiling water, if needed, to cover. Cook in the oven at 100C/200F/gas low for 8 hours. Top up with more boiling water as needed, and push the knuckle down into the beans. Discard the bones and rind and stir chunks of the bacon meat into the beans. Season with salt and pepper to taste.
   This dish is traditionally served with Boston brown bread (page 139).

ORANGE AND TARRAGON GAMMON STEAKS

4 gammon steaks, about
   175 g/6 oz each
50 g/2 oz butter
2 oranges
45 ml/3 tbls clear honey
15 ml/1 tbls chopped fresh
   tarragon, or 10 ml/2 tsp
   dried tarragon

Serves 4

Snip all round the gammon rind to prevent it from curling.
Place the steaks in a grill pan and dot with half of the butter.
Cook under a moderately hot grill for 5 minutes, turn and dot
with the remaining butter. Broil for a further 5 minutes.
   Grate the rind of the oranges, peel them and cut them into
slices. Transfer the gammon to a heated serving dish and keep
it warm. Stir in the orange rind, honey and tarragon into the
juices in the pan, add the orange slices and heat under the
grill, turning them once. Arrange the orange slices on the
gammon and pour over the honey sauce. Serve with French
fried potatoes.

BACON HOTPOT

Photograph opposite

A real "homestead" dish.

750 g/1½ lb collar of bacon
40 g/1½ oz butter
1 medium onion, thinly sliced
4 medium leeks, well washed
   and sliced
30 ml/2 tbls flour
450 ml/¾ pt chicken stock
   (page 12)
2 medium carrots, thinly
   sliced
pepper
250 g/8 oz can butter beans,
   drained
30 ml/2 tbls chopped parsley
30 ml/2 tbls double cream

Serves 4

Cut off rind and excess fat from bacon and cut the meat into
2.5-cm/1-in cubes. Put them in a pan, cover with cold water,
bring to the boil and drain. Toss the meat to dry on kitchen
paper.
   Melt the butter in a flameproof casserole and fry the onion
and leeks over moderate heat for 3 minutes, stirring once or
twice. Sprinkle on the flour, stir well and slowly pour on the
stock, stirring. Bring to the boil, and simmer for 2 minutes.
Add the carrots and bacon squares, season with pepper and
return to the boil. Cover and simmer for 1 hour. Add the butter
beans and continue simmering for 15 minutes. Finally, stir in
the parsley and cream.

4: HIGHDAYS AND HOLIDAYS

Whenever there is something to celebrate – a festival, a holiday, or just because the family is all together again, food plays a major part in the proceedings. It is unthinkable to celebrate Thanksgiving Day without the traditional turkey and all the trimmings, or to let Independence Day go past without a special meal of some kind.

These are not usually times for experimenting with new recipes. Tradition takes a firm hand, and the familiarity of the same dishes, served year after year for generations, breeds contentment.

Thanksgiving Day, commemorating the 17th-century Pilgrims' first celebration, takes the form of a harvest festival. The Pilgrims, overcoming incredible hardship and successfully raising crops of corn, beans and squash, and having learned how to hunt wild turkeys, decided that, "We might after a more special manner rejoice together, after we had gathered the fruit of our labors". They went on to record that four men in one day killed enough wild fowl to feed the whole company for a week - which rings strangely true of many a refrigerator and ice-box the day before the national holiday nowadays!

Our Thanksgiving menu has turkey with rice and cranberry stuffing, and cranberry sauce, beautifully rich color contrasts to the golden poultry, candied sweet potatoes, a quick-to-make Succotash – that life-saving mixture of corn and beans – and the inevitable pumpkin pie, with apple pie and ice cream for good measure.

Poached salmon has been traditional fare for the other great American national holiday, Independence Day on the Fourth of July, since the First Lady of America, Abigail Adams, served it at the White House in 1776. Then it was accompanied by the new season's vegetables – tiny potatoes and peas – and an egg sauce. For a celebration buffet, the salmon could be served cold with mayonnaise and a salad selection.

The Fourth of July also offers a great chance for outdoor celebrations, a party on the terrace or a barbecue on the beach. In Southern style, we have put together a meal with shrimp and okra gumbo, and chicken and ham jambalaya which, according to your spirit of adventure, can either be cooked at home and ferried in vacuum jugs to the picnic site, or prepared, old-style, over an open fire or camping stove.

The other menu to serve under the sun or stars can be a joint affair. Someone can bring the deviled chicken drumsticks, other friends contribute the corncobs, anchovy bread, chocolate browns, fruit cocktail and the clams.

Ah, the clams! Our recipe for clams on the rack pays lip-service to the way they are cooked at a large clambake in the sand on the seashore. That's when they have a bakemaster to do it in style. He digs huge pits in the sand, lines them with stones and covers them with maple twigs and more stones. The wood burns, the stones get hot and on go clumps of wet seaweed to produce the steam. Wire-mesh trays of clams are piled on top, with trays of corn cobs and whole potatoes above them. A tarpaulin keeps in the steam, and an hour-and-a-half later – come and get it!

With turkey given pride of place in the autumn festivities, we have opted for goose for the Christmas celebrations. Rum punch, goose, an ice cream and fruit bombe, and the booziest cake-cum-pudding ever. Oh, and little take-home chocolate boxes for children's parties.

Happy holidays!

SUMMER BARBECUE
DEVILLED CHICKEN DRUMSTICKS

The chicken can be marinated and coated, ready to cook on a barbecue, or cooked in advance and carried for a picnic.

6 large chicken drumsticks
50 g/2 oz breadcrumbs
25 g/1 oz ground almonds
Marinade
90 ml/6 tbls vegetable oil
30 ml/2 tbls red wine vinegar
10 ml/2 tsp Madras curry
   powder
30 ml/2 tbls mango sauce
10 ml/2 tsp Worcestershire
   sauce
salt and pepper

Serves 6

Mix together all the ingredients for the marinade. Slash the chicken legs at intervals and place them in the marinade. Set aside, turning them frequently, for 2 hours.

   Broil the drumsticks for 10 minutes, brushing them frequently with the marinade. Mix together the breadcrumbs and almonds and toss the chicken to coat them thoroughly. Broil them, turning frequently, for a further 15-20 minutes. Serve hot or cold, with Spiced tomato sauce (page 168).

CLAMS ON THE RACK

It takes time and expertise to set up a clam bake – here's a scaled-down version that is good with mussels, too.

3.5 liters/6 pt fresh clams or
   mussels
50 g/2 oz butter
1 large onion, finely chopped
3 cloves garlic, crushed
4 small celery stalks, thinly
   sliced
a few stalks of parsley
2 bay leaves
300 ml/½ pt dry white wine
150 ml/¼ pt dry vermouth
90 ml/6 tbls double cream
salt and pepper
45 ml/3 tbls chopped parsley

Serves 6

Wash the clams or mussels in a bucket of fresh water, changing it frequently. Scrub them thoroughly and discard any which have opened or which float on the water.

   Melt the butter in a large pan and cook the onion, garlic and celery over low heat for 10 minutes, stirring occasionally. Add the parsley, bay leaves, wine, vermouth and cream and season well with salt and pepper. Add the shellfish, bring to the boil and, stirring frequently, simmer for 10 minutes, or until the shells open. Discard any that remain closed.

   Lift the shellfish with a draining spoon and divide them between 6 deep serving bowls. Boil the sauce for 2 minutes, strain it into a jug, adjust seasoning and serve separately.

CHICKEN AND HAM JAMBALAYA

Photograph on page 68

Any similarity between this rice dish and Paella is more than coincidental - France ceded Louisiana to Spain in 1762 and the Spanish brought their own cooking techniques and spices to the region.

1.5 kg/3¼ lb chicken
250 g/8 oz ham
30 ml/2 tbls vegetable oil
2 large onions, chopped
4 celery stalks, thinly sliced
1 green pepper, seeded and
   sliced
275 g/9 oz long-grain rice
900 ml/1½ pt chicken stock
   (page 12)
salt and pepper
2.5 ml/½ tsp cayenne
2.5 ml/½ tsp dried oregano

Serves 4-6

Skin the chicken and discard the skin. Cut all the meat from the bones and cut it into bite-sized pieces. You can make the chicken stock with the giblets and carcass. Trim the fat from the ham and cut the meat into 2-cm/¾-in cubes. Heat the oil in a large, shallow pan and fry the onions and celery over moderate heat for 3 – 4 minutes, stirring once or twice Add the chicken, ham and pepper and fry, stirring frequently, for 10 minutes, until the ingredients are evenly golden brown. Stir in the rice, add the stock, season well with salt and pepper and stir in the cayenne and oregano.

   Bring to the boil, stir once, cover the pan and simmer over very low heat for 45 minutes, stirring occasionally. Uncover the pan and cook over moderate heat, stirring frequently to dry the rice.

PINO COLADO

Photograph on page 69

White rum, cream and pineapple juice – the perfect recipe for a carefree day.

1 liter/1¾ pt pineapple juice,
   chilled
300 ml/½ pt double cream,
   chilled
250 ml/9 fl oz white rum
2.5 ml/½ tsp coconut essence
   or flavoring or 60 ml/4 tbls
   Malibu
crushed ice
maraschino cherries, to
   decorate

Makes 8-10 glasses

Thoroughly blend the fruit juice and cream and stir in the rum and coconut flavoring or liqueur. Pour over a little crushed ice in chilled glasses. Decorate with maraschino cherries.

CHOCOLATE BROWNIES

No matter how generous the portions, there's always room at an outdoor party for something chocolatey to nibble. These little squares are just the thing.

75 g/3 oz plain chocolate
75 g/3 oz butter
300 g/10 oz caster sugar
3 eggs, lightly beaten
a pinch of salt
125 g/4 oz flour
125 g/4 oz walnuts, chopped
7.5 ml/1½ tsp vanilla essence

Makes 16 cakes

Melt the chocolate and butter in the top of a double boiler or a bowl fitted over a pan of simmering water. Remove from the heat and beat in the sugar, egg, salt, flour, walnuts and vanilla.

Spoon the mixture into a baking tin 22.5-cm/9-in square and level the top. Bake in the oven at 180C/350F/gas 4 for 40 minutes, until the cake is springy to the touch. Cool on a wire rack and cut into squares.

SOUTHERN-STYLE PICNIC
NEW ORLEANS SHRIMP GUMBO

Photograph on page 68

Outdoor cooks can prepare this dish, old-style, on a picnic stove outside a camper; others can bring it to the party ready-made, in vacuum jars.

25 g/1 oz butter
30 ml/2 tbls vegetable oil
3 large onions, sliced
2 cloves garlic, finely chopped
1 green pepper, seeded and
   sliced
1 red pepper, seeded and
   sliced
400 g/14 oz can okra, drained,
   rinsed and sliced
450 g/15 oz can tomatoes
1 liter/1¾ pt chicken stock
   (page 12)
salt and pepper
1.5 ml/¼ tsp cayenne pepper
200 g/7 oz long-grain rice
250 g/8 oz peeled shrimps or
   prawns

Serves 6

Melt the butter and oil and fry the onions over moderate heat for 3 minutes, stirring occasionally. Add the garlic, green and red pepper and fry, stirring once or twice, for a further 3 minutes. Add the okra, tomatoes with the juice from the can, and the stock, and season with salt, pepper and cayenne. Bring to the boil, cover and simmer for 30 minutes. Add the rice, bring back to the boil and simmer for 10 minutes. Add the shrimps or prawns, adjust seasoning and simmer for a further 10 minutes.

Serve the gumbo in deep bowls, with plenty of hot, crusty bread.

JELLIED TOMATO SALAD

Photograph on page 68, foreground

You can take these jellied molds in an insulated bag and turn them out on to picnic plates. They make a colorful salad accompaniment.

450 ml/¾ pt tomato juice
15 ml/1 tbls tomato purée
75 g/3 oz raspberry jelly
   tablets
30 ml/2 tbls red wine vinegar
5 ml/1 tsp lemon juice
5 ml/1 tsp caster sugar
salt and pepper
30 ml/2 tbls cucumber, seeded
   and finely chopped
shredded lettuce leaves, to
   serve

Serves 4

Bring the tomato juice to the boil and stir in the purée until it is well blended. Remove from the heat and stir in the jelly tablets until they have dissolved. Add the vinegar, lemon juice and sugar and season well with salt and pepper.

Place a few pieces of cucumber in the base of four 150 ml/ ¼ pt lidded jelly molds and pour on the jelly. Leave to cool, then cover and chill in the refrigerator for about 1 hour, to set. Serve garnished with shredded lettuce.

CITRUS COCKTAIL

Photograph on page 69

Whether your barbecue is at high noon or as the sun goes down, this is a perfect appetizer.

150 ml/¼ pt Grand Marnier
juice of 4 oranges
juice of 1 lemon
juice of 1 grapefruit
40 g/1½ oz caster sugar
300 ml/½ pt lemonade
crushed ice
orange slices, maraschino
   cherries and mint sprigs, to
   decorate

Makes 8 glasses

Mix together the liqueur, fruit juices and sugar and pour into the lemonade. Stir and pour over crushed ice. Decorate each glass with a "kebab" of sliced orange, cherries and mint.

GARLIC AND ANCHOVY BREAD

Have the loaf split, spread and wrapped, ready to heat over the fire.

1 French loaf
125 g/4 oz unsalted butter,
  softened
1 clove garlic, crushed
4 canned anchovy fillets,
  drained and chopped
30 ml/2 tbls chopped chervil
  or parsley

Serves 8

Split the loaf diagonally into 2.5-cm/1-in slices, without cutting right through. Beat the butter and beat in the garlic, anchovy and herb. Spread the bread on both sides of each slit. Wrap it closely in foil. Heat on the grill for 20 minutes, turning it often.

BARBECUED CORN ON THE COB

This is the simplest first course ever, to eat round the fire while the meat is sizzling.

6 large corn cobs
175 g/6 oz unsalted butter,
  softened
1 clove garlic, crushed
30 ml/2 tbls chopped parsley
4 spring onions, finely
  chopped
salt and pepper

Serves 6

Strip away the corn husk and silk and trim the ends of the cobs. Beat the butter and beat in the garlic, parsley and onions and season well with salt and pepper.

Spread each corn cob all round with the butter and place each one in the center of a double layer of foil. Wrap the foil to enclose the corn completely, making secure the joins. Cook the corn in the ashes for 15-20 minutes, turning the parcels frequently. Serve piping hot.

THANKSGIVING
THANKSGIVING TURKEY WITH RICE AND CRANBERRY STUFFING

Photograph on page 64

For the annual feast-day, a golden bird filled with a colorful mixture of rice and berries.

5 kg/11 lb turkey, dressed
  weight
½ lemon
salt and pepper
12 thin slices streaky bacon
250 g/8 oz butter
150 ml/¼ pt dry white wine,
  or cider
Gravy
the giblets of the turkey
1 onion, sliced
a few stalks of parsley
6 black peppercorns
a pinch of sugar
2 bay leaves
30 ml/2 tbls flour
Stuffing
375 g/12 oz long-grain rice
125 g/4 oz butter
1 large onion, finely chopped
30 ml/2 tbls chopped parsley
10 ml/2 tsp dried thyme
a pinch of ground cloves
a pinch of grated nutmeg
2 × 185 g/6½ oz jars cranberry
  sauce

Serves 12-14

First prepare the giblet stock and the stuffing. These can be done in advance. Put all the giblets except the liver in a pan with the onion, parsley, peppercorns, sugar and bay leaves, cover with water and bring to the boil. Cover the pan and simmer for 1 hour. Strain into a bowl, skim off fat and set aside.

To make the stuffing, cook the rice in a large pan of boiling, salted water for about 12 minutes, or until it is just tender. Drain in a colander, pour hot water over it and drain again. Melt the butter and fry the onion over moderate heat for 4 minutes, stirring once or twice. Remove from the heat and stir in the rice, herbs, spices and cranberry sauce. Season with salt and pepper. Leave to cool.

Wash and dry the turkey inside and out. Pack the stuffing into the cavity and sew up the bird. Rub the skin with the lemon and season well with salt and pepper. Cover the breast with bacon rashers. Place the bird in a roasting pan. Melt the butter in a small pan, pour on the wine and pour over the turkey. Cover the pan with foil.

Cook in the oven at 220C/425F/gas 7 for 20 minutes. Reduce the heat to 170C/325F/gas 3 and cook for a further 3¾ hours, basting frequently. Remove the foil and the bacon rashers and cook the bird uncovered for a further 30 minutes, or until the skin is crisp and golden brown and the turkey is well cooked. To test, pierce the thick part of the thigh with a fine skewer. The juices should run clear.

Transfer the turkey to a heated serving dish, cover with foil and keep it warm. Skim the fat from the pan, chop the liver and stir it into the juices. Stir 30 ml/2 tbls of the juices into the flour and stir them into the pan. Pour on 150 ml/¼ pt of the giblet stock, season with salt and pepper, bring to the boil and simmer for 3 minutes. Serve separately.

CRANBERRY SAUCE

Buy the sauce bottled or canned, or make your own and chill or freeze it. But whatever you do, don't forget it!

500 g/1 lb sugar
grated rind and juice of 1
  orange
500 g/1 lb whole cranberries,
  fresh or frozen

Makes 900 ml/1½ pt sauce

Put 450 ml/¾ pt water into a pan, add the sugar and stir over low heat until it has dissolved. Bring to the boil and boil for 5 minutes. Add the orange rind and juice and the cranberries, stir carefully with a wooden spoon and simmer for 5 minutes, until the berries are bright red and the sauce is translucent. Leave to cool.
  Store in a lidded container. Serve with roast turkey, goose and ham, and with cold poultry, ham and other meats.

CANDIED SWEET POTATOES

The American Indians cultivated sweet potatoes and yams, vegetables native to the tropical areas of the Continent, and the Pilgrims discovered them – thankfully.

6 medium sweet potatoes
salt
175 g/6 oz light Muscovado
  sugar
50 g/2 oz butter
125 g/4 oz white
  marshmallows

Serves 6

Cook the potatoes in boiling, salted water until tender. Peel them, slice thickly and sprinkle with salt. In a flameproof dish, mix together the sugar, 150 ml/¼ pt water and the butter. Dissolve over low heat, and bring to the boil. Add the potatoes and stir them in the syrup over moderate heat until the liquid has evaporated and the vegetable is covered with a thick toffee-like coating. Scatter the marshmallows on top and toast under a hot grill.

PUMPKIN PIE

Photograph on page 80

A "must" for every Thanksgiving dinner since the very first one.

1×25-cm/10-in unbaked
  sweet shortcrust pastry
  case (page 105)
1 kg/2¼ lb pumpkin, peeled,
  seeded and diced
125 g/4 oz light Muscovado
  sugar
3 eggs
5 ml/1 tsp ground cinnamon
2.5 ml/½ tsp grated nutmeg
5 ml/1 tsp ground ginger
a pinch of ground cloves
a pinch of salt
300 ml/½ pt single cream

Serves 6-8

Steam the pumpkin for 20 minutes, or until it is tender, then mash it. Beat together the sugar and eggs and stir in the spices, salt and cream. Add the pumpkin and beat until smooth.
  Pour the filling into the pastry case. Bake in the oven at 200C/400F/gas 6 for 40 minutes, or until the filling is set. Serve warm, with whipped cream or soured cream.

SUCCOTASH

This dish of lima, or broad, beans and sweetcorn comes from the Narraganset Indians and the name from "msaksatas," which means something broken into pieces. It is a truly indigenous dish and one which the Settlers adopted.

500 g/1 lb can lima, or broad
  beans, drained
500 g/1 lb can sweetcorn
  kernels, drained
50 g/2 oz butter
1 medium onion, finely
  chopped
2.5 ml/½ tsp salt
5 ml/1 tsp caster sugar
1.5 ml/¼ tsp ground pepper
150 ml/¼ pt chicken stock
  (page 12)
15 ml/1 tbls chopped parsley,
  to garnish, optional

Serves 6-8

Melt the butter and fry the onion over moderate heat for 4 minutes, stirring occasionally. Add the beans, corn, seasonings and stock. Bring to the boil and simmer, uncovered, for 10 minutes. Turn on to a heated serving dish and garnish with the parsley.

POACHED SALMON WITH ORANGE HOLLANDAISE SAUCE

Photograph opposite

In 1776 John Adams, second President of the United States, served poached salmon at an Independence Day celebration, and the fish has been associated with the occasion ever since.

1.5 kg/3¼ lb piece salmon,
   cleaned
2 thin slices of lemon
1 carrot, thinly sliced
1 medium onion, sliced
2 bay leaves
a few stalks of parsley
4 black peppercorns
Sauce
15 ml/1 tbls orange juice
salt and pepper
4 large egg yolks
250 g/8 oz unsalted butter,
   diced
5 ml/1 tsp grated orange rind

Serves 6-8

Put the lemon, carrot, onion, bay leaves, parsley and peppercorns in a fish kettle or large pan, half filled with water, and bring to the boil. Simmer for 10 minutes. Lower in the fish on a rack or trivet, bring back to the boil and simmer for 20 minutes. Lift from the pan, drain thoroughly on kitchen towelling and place on a heated dish.

To make the sauce, put the orange juice into the top of a double boiler or a bowl fitted over a pan of simmering water, add 15 ml/1 tbls water and season with salt and pepper. Add the egg yolks and a cube of butter and whisk well. Continue adding the butter piece by piece, whisking all the time. Beat the sauce until smooth, add the orange rind and adjust seasoning.

Pour a little sauce over the salmon to garnish and serve the remainder separately.

STRAWBERRY ICE CREAM ROLL

Memories of Independence Day parties drift back to the time when strawberry ice cream was made in a churn, and everyone took a turn at cranking the handle – even on the beach. The method is simpler now, but its popularity lingers on.

175 g/6 oz caster sugar
500 g/1 lb strawberries,
   hulled, or frozen ones,
   thawed
150 ml/¼ pt redcurrant juice
15 ml/1 tbls orange juice
450 ml/¾ pt double cream,
   whipped
a few fresh strawberries, to
   decorate

Serves 6-8

Put the sugar in the pan with 150 ml/¼ pt water, bring to the boil, stirring occasionally to dissolve the sugar, and boil for 5 minutes. Leave the syrup to cool.

Purée the strawberries in a blender and mix with the redcurrant juice and orange juice. Stir in the cooled syrup and gradually fold in 300 ml/½ pt of the cream. Pour the mixture into freezing trays, cover and freeze for 1 hour.

Turn the mixture into a chilled bowl and whisk until it is smooth. Pour it into a washed 1 kg/2 lb used can, cover the end with foil and stand it upright in the freezer. Freeze for 3 hours.

To serve, wrap the can for a few seconds in a tea towel wrung out in hot water and unmold on to a dish. Pipe the remaining cream to decorate and arrange the fresh strawberries. Leave in the main part of the refrigerator for 30 minutes before serving.

MINT JULEP

Two hundred and more years of independence calls for a toast. This one is long and very refreshing.

a handful of fresh, young
   mint leaves
45 ml/3 tbls caster sugar
cracked ice
450 ml/¾ pt bourbon
   whiskey, chilled
12 sprigs of mint, to garnish

Serves 6

Put the mint leaves in a jug, add the sugar and 30 ml/2 tbls water. Stir with a wooden spoon to dissolve the sugar and crush the mint leaves. Leave in the refrigerator for 1 hour, then strain into a glass serving jug. Fill the jug with cracked ice, pour on the whiskey and stir well. Chill for 30 minutes.

Pour into 6 tumblers and garnish each one with 2 mint sprigs. Serve with drinking straws.

CHRISTMAS
ROAST GOOSE WITH SPICED FRUIT STUFFING

With turkey enjoyed and venerated at Thanksgiving, roast goose makes a perfect choice for the Christmas festivities.

4.5 kg/10 lb goose, dressed
   weight
salt and pepper
1 kg/2¼ lb potatoes, peeled
   and thickly sliced
2 large onions, sliced into
   rings
Gravy
the giblets from the bird,
   washed
1 medium onion, sliced
1 *bouquet garni*
4 black peppercorns
30 ml/2 tbls flour
200 ml/7 fl oz dry white wine
Stuffing
50 g/2 oz butter
1 medium onion, finely
   chopped
1 clove garlic, crushed
250 g/8 oz streaky bacon, rind
   removed, chopped
2 celery stalks, finely chopped
2 dessert apples, peeled,
   cored and chopped
50 g/2 oz seedless raisins
75 g/3 oz breadcrumbs
50 g/2 oz walnuts, chopped
2.5 ml/½ tsp dried sage
2.5 ml/½ tsp mixed ground
   spice
1.5 ml/¼ tsp grated nutmeg
15 ml/1 tbls clear honey

Serves 6-8

Trim the goose by removing any feathers and quills. Remove the long wing pinions. Wash and dry the bird inside and out and remove any large pieces of fat.

To make the giblet stock for the gravy, put the giblets into a pan with the onion, *bouquet garni* and peppercorns, cover with water, bring to the boil, and simmer for 1 hour. Strain and skim off the fat. Set aside. The stock can be made in advance.

To make the stuffing, melt the butter and fry the onion, garlic and bacon over moderate heat for 4-5 minutes, stirring frequently. Add the celery and apple and fry for a further 2 minutes. Remove from the heat and stir in the raisins, breadcrumbs, walnuts, sage, spices and honey. Season with salt and pepper. Leave to cool, then pack into the goose.

Secure the vent with a skewer. Prick all over the goose skin with a fork to release the fat as it cooks. Season well with salt and pepper. Stand the goose on a rack in a roasting pan. Place in the oven at 220C/425F/gas 7 for 20 minutes. Pour off the fat, reduce the heat to 180C/350F/gas 4 and cook for a further 2½ hours. Pour off all except 60 ml/4 tbls of the fat.

Place the potatoes and onions in a single layer in the pan and season with salt and pepper. Replace the rack and the bird and continue cooking for 1¼ hours, pouring off excess fat once or twice.

Transfer the goose to a heated serving plate and keep it warm. Pour off fat from the tin. Brown the potatoes and onions under a hot grill and transfer them to a heated serving dish.

To make the gravy, stir the flour into 30 ml/2 tbls of fat in the pan and cook over moderate heat for 3 minutes. Pour on 300 ml/½ pt of the giblet stock and the wine, stir well and season with salt and pepper. Bring to the boil and simmer for 5 minutes. Serve separately.

ICE CREAM BOMBE

A spectacular dessert, perfect after poultry-and-all-the-trimmings at Christmastime. And in the summer too!

600 ml/1 pt lemon sorbet
   (page 113)
450 ml/¾ pt meringue ice
   cream (page 112)
250 g/8 oz frozen raspberries,
   thawed
150 ml/¼ pt double cream,
   whipped, to decorate

Serves 8

Chill a 1.5-liter/2½-pt pudding bowl. Transfer the sorbet to the main part of the refrigerator for about 30 minutes to soften. Spread the sorbet to line the bowl with a 2.5-cm/1-in layer. Cover with foil and freeze for 1 hour. Transfer the meringue ice cream to the refrigerator to soften.

Stir the raspberries into the ice cream. Spoon into the bowl and smooth the top. Cover with foil and freeze for at least 2 hours.

To serve, turn the bombe on to a serving dish. Pipe rosettes of cream around the edge and to decorate the top. Leave in the refrigerator for 30 minutes before serving.

RUM PUNCH

This is the kind of drink that seems to melt the frost!

1 × 75 cl bottle dark rum
juice of 2 oranges
juice of 1 lemon
250 g/8 oz can pineapple
   cubes, with juice
100 ml/3½ fl oz orange wine
1 orange, thinly sliced
1 lemon
12 cloves
60 ml/4 tbls sugar
1.5 liter/2½ pt soda water
cracked ice, to serve

Makes about 16 drinks

Mix the rum, orange juice, lemon juice, pineapple, orange wine, sliced orange and the lemon stuck with the cloves. Stir in the sugar and leave to infuse for about 2 hours. Stir in the soda water just before serving. Pour over cracked ice in tumblers.

CHAMPAGNE PUNCH

For this and any other celebration, a bubbly, fruity punch gets everyone in the party spirit.

1×75 cl bottle dry white wine
150 ml/¼ pt peach nectar
15 ml/1 tbls lemon juice
100 ml/3/½ fl oz brandy
1 × 75 cl bottle Champagne,
   or other sparkling white
   wine
3-4 peaches, stoned and
   sliced, to decorate

Makes 20-24 glasses

Put the white wine, peach nectar, lemon juice and brandy into a bowl and stir to mix well. Chill in the refrigerator for at least 1 hour. Just before serving, pour on the Champagne and add the peach slices.

CREOLE CHRISTMAS CAKE

Photograph on page 77

This is the booziest, moistest, richest cake ever. Serve it with whipped cream and liqueurs or coffee. For best results, start it a week ahead so that the flavors can blend.

100 ml/3½ fl oz dark rum
100 ml/3½ fl oz brandy
100 ml/3½ fl oz port
100 ml/3½ fl oz cherry brandy
15 ml/1 tbls Angostura bitters
5 ml/1 tsp ground cinnamon
5 ml/1 tsp ground nutmeg
5 ml/1 tsp salt
5 ml/1 tsp ground cloves
15 ml/1 tbls vanilla essence
30 ml/2 tbls molasses sugar
1 kg/2¼ lb seedless raisins
500 g/1 lb currants
250 g/8 oz stoned prunes
125 g/4 oz glacé cherries
250 g/8 oz chopped mixed
   peel
125 g/4 oz Brazil nuts,
   chopped
10 eggs
500 g/1 lb butter
500 g/1 lb self-raising flour
750 g/1½ lb demerara sugar

Serves 12-16

Put the rum, brandy, port, cherry brandy, bitters and 100 ml/3 ½ fl oz water into a large pan. Add the spices, salt, vanilla, molasses sugar, dried fruits, peel and nuts. Stir well and bring slowly to simmering point. Simmer, without boiling, for 15 minutes. If you have time to plan ahead, pour the mixture into a container, cool, cover and store.

   Beat together the eggs and butter, gradually sift in the flour and stir in the sugar. Beat well until the mixture is smooth. Stir into the fruit mixture. Pour into a greased and lined 22.5-cm/9-in baking tin and cover with a double layer of greaseproof paper.

   Bake in the oven at 140C/275F/gas 1 for 3-3½ hours, until cooked. The cake will still be moist in the center. Cool in the tin, then turn onto a wire rack. When cold, wrap in foil to store.

CHRISTMAS CHOCOLATE BOXES

Photograph on page 76

These little chocolate boxes with their crunchy, spongy filling look pretty on the Christmas table. Wrapped in clingfilm, they can be hung on the tree, or offered as trick-or-treat presents at Hallowe'en.

350 g/12 oz plain chocolate
125 g/4 oz margarine
125 g/4 oz caster sugar
2 eggs, lightly beaten
125 g/4 oz self-raising flour
30 ml/2 tbls orange juice
50 g/2 oz crunchy nut corn
   flakes
grated rind of ½ orange
Filling and topping
125 g/4 oz butter, softened
300 g/10 oz icing sugar
15 ml/1 tbls orange juice

Makes 9 chocolate boxes

Melt the chocolate in a bowl over a pan of hot water, or in the top of a double boiler. Pour it on to a sheet of waxed paper and spread to a thin, even layer about 45.5×25.5 cm/18×10 in. Mark out into 45×5-cm/2-in squares and chill in the refrigerator.

   Cream together the margarine and sugar and beat in the egg a little at a time. Fold in half of the flour, beat in the orange juice and add the remaining flour. Stir in the corn flakes and orange rind. Spoon the mixture into a greased and lined 18-cm/7-in square sandwich tin and level the top.

   Bake in the oven at 180C/350F/gas 4 for 40 minutes, until the cake is springy and golden brown. Cool slightly in the tin, then turn out on to a wire rack to cool. Trim the edges and cut into 9-cm/2-in squares.

   To make butter icing, cream the butter, sift in 250 g/8 oz of the icing sugar and beat in the orange juice. Spread the butter icing on to 5 sides of the sponge squares. Break the chocolate into the marked squares and press one on to each "buttered" side of the sponge.

   Add a little water to the remaining icing sugar to make the glacé icing. Spoon it into a small icing bag fitted with a small, plain nozzle. Pipe the icing on to the chocolate squares with a bow on top, to represent tied-up parcels.

DOUBLE-CRUST APPLE PIE

Apple pie and ice cream, a popular favorite for every highday and holiday.

450 g/14 oz shortcrust pastry
   (page 105)
750 g/1½ lb cooking apples,
   peeled, cored and sliced
75 g/3 oz light Muscovado
   sugar
5 ml/1 tsp cornflour
grated rind and juice of 1
   orange
1.5 ml/¼ tsp ground
   cinnamon
15 g/½ oz butter, diced
milk, for brushing
30 ml/2 tbls granulated sugar

Serves 6

Divide the pastry in half. On a lightly-floured board roll out one piece and use it to line a 20-cm/8-in greased pie plate. Mix together the apples, sugar, cornflour, cinnamon and orange rind and juice and spread over the pastry base. Scatter with butter. Roll out the second piece of pastry. Brush the edges of the case with milk. Cover with the pastry lid and brush the top with milk. Reroll the trimmings, cut them into leaf shapes and arrange in a pattern. Brush with milk and sprinkle the pie with sugar.
   Bake in the oven at 220C/425F/gas 7 for 15 minutes. Reduce the heat to 180C/350F/gas 4 and cook for a further 25 minutes, or until the top is golden brown.
   Serve warm or cold, with ice cream.

5:VEGETABLES AND SALADS

America has been described as the vegetable basket of the world - acres and acres of luscious cultivated vegetables stretching from coast to coast, as far as the mind's eye can envisage. A miraculous country for vegetarians!

California, with its mild climate and fertile valleys, is the most plentiful producer and, like Florida, enjoys an almost perpetual summer. It leads the USA in an impressive shopping list of vegetable crops – asparagus, avocados, broccoli, carrots, globe artichokes, lettuces and tomatoes, as well as in oranges, peaches and pears – and wines from its grapes, of course. But then every State and region has its proud claim to cropping achievements, and the various State agricultural and horticultural boards compete with each other like so many market stallholders shouting their irresistible wares.

American family cooks are imaginative in their preparation of vegetables; just how imaginative I was to discover in the course of a single evening. I asked a group of American wives for their favorite ways of serving leaf and root vegetables and salads and, the next thing I knew, I was their guest at a "bring a dish" buffet supper.

The cooks clubbed together to provide a huge dish of prawns as the centerpiece for the first course, and baskets of barbecued chicken to follow. Then each one brought a salad dish as an "opener," or a hot vegetable accompaniment. What interested me was that the girls brought their salads to the party in insulated bags and boxes to keep them cool on the journey just as diligently as others did the same, to keep their dishes hot.

To sample with our giant Pacific prawns, Cheryl, from New Hampshire, brought a coleslaw salad with caraway seeds and soured cream dressing. Audrey from Dakota contributed vegetarian pasta salad with corn, celery and mushrooms, and

Betty, a Washington lady, took on the task of creating the well-known Caesar salad with garlic croutons. From Georgia, Mary served little scoops of avocado tossed in a peanut dressing, Kim from Texas dug into her mother's cookbook for pinto salad with hard-boiled eggs and cheese, and Jean, an Arkansas lass, made the most delicious rice salad I have ever eaten, with black olives, green grapes, raisins and pecans. Chris, from Ohio, reminded us of the strong German influence with her potato, bacon and celery salad, and Phyll brought a touch of Massachusetts sophistication with an elegant molded asparagus salad. And we still had the main course to come!

A tiny spoonful at a time, I noted Pat's contribution from California, a broccoli and cream cheese casserole; sherried Brussels sprouts cooked with cinnamon and soured cream to a recipe which Roberta had brought from New York, and creamed cabbage which Jan had prepared the Kansas way. Dana, from Oregon, had brought a bowl of lemon sauce and crisp golden aubergine and mushroom fritters to dip into it, and Alyce, from Louisiana, produced an okra pilaff to a recipe little changed since the Africans arrived to work on the rice plantations. Ethel's contribution from Arizona was a corn, bean and squash casserole tinglingly seasoned with chillies, which went extremely well with Barbara's hot corn cakes. A Nebraska lady, well used to portable feasts, she unwrapped them piping hot from countless layers of foil.

But top marks for presentation went to Dee, from Alabama. She poured warm brandy over her dish of sweet potatoes and brought it to the table in a mass of blue flames!

I can bring you these and other favorite salad and vegetable recipes. I only wish I could convey the warm friendliness of that cooks' get-together evening.

BROCCOLI CASSEROLE

The Lower Rio Grande Valley is described as the "biggest winter vegetable basket" of Texas, with broccoli, a prime crop, harvested from late November through to March. Here's a delicious vegetarian way to serve it.

500 g/1 lb broccoli
3 medium onions, chopped
salt
75 g/3 oz butter
30 ml/2 tbls flour
225 ml/8 fl oz milk
75 g/3 oz full-fat cream cheese
a large pinch of grated
   nutmeg
pepper
50 g/2 oz day-old white
   breadcrumbs
125 g/4 oz grated hard cheese

Serves 4

Cook the broccoli and onion in a little salted water for 10 minutes, or until just tender. Drain.

Melt 25 g/1 oz of the butter in a pan, stir in the flour and gradually pour on the milk. Bring to the boil, stirring, and simmer for 3 minutes. Remove from heat, stir in the cream cheese and nutmeg and season the sauce with salt and pepper. Stir the sauce into the broccoli and onion and turn into a greased ovenproof dish.

Melt the remaining butter, stir in the breadcrumbs and 25 g/1 oz of the cheese. Spread the remaining cheese over the broccoli and top with the breadcrumbs. Bake in the oven at 180C/350F/gas 4 for 30 minutes. Serve very hot. This dish can be completely assembled in advance, and left ready to bake.

CORN, BEAN AND SQUASH CASSEROLE

This one-pot meal is developed from a dish of the Indian Hopi tribe, from America's Southwest. Dried pinto beans were originally combined with the corn; fresh or frozen broad (lima) beans and French beans give a lighter result.

30 ml/2 tbls vegetable oil
500 g/1 lb courgettes
   (zucchini) or other squash,
   trimmed and sliced
350 g/12 oz onions, sliced
2 cloves garlic, finely chopped
1 red chilli, seeded and finely
   chopped
300 ml/½ pt chicken stock
   (page 12)
250 g/8 oz corn kernels
500 g/1 lb shelled broad (lima)
   beans, fresh or frozen and
   thawed
250 g/8 oz French beans,
   topped, tailed and cut into
   2.5-cm/1-in slices or frozen
   beans, thawed
500 g/1 lb tomatoes, skinned
   and chopped
salt and pepper

Serves 8

Heat the oil in a large flameproof casserole and fry the courgettes, onions and garlic over moderate heat for 4-5 minutes, stirring often. Add the chilli, stock, corn kernels and beans, bring to the boil and simmer for 10 minutes. Add the tomatoes, season with salt and pepper and simmer for a further 5 minutes, or until all the vegetables are tender. Taste and adjust seasoning if needed.

(As an alternative, canned and drained white haricot beans or butter beans may be substituted for the broad beans.)

AUBERGINE (EGG PLANT) FRITTERS WITH LEMON SAUCE

You can serve these crisp-on-the-outside fritters to accompany roast or grilled meat, but they are so good they deserve a slot of their own.

2 large aubergines (egg
    plants), cut into 6-mm/¼-
    in slices
coarse salt
45 ml/3 tbls vegetable oil
125 g/4 oz flour
200 ml/7 fl oz tepid water
1 egg white, beaten
oil, for deep frying
Lemon sauce
75 ml/5 tbls lemon juice
250 g/8 oz butter, cut into
    small pieces
15 ml/1 tbls chopped chives
salt and pepper

Serves 4

Put the aubergines into a colander over a bowl, sprinkle them with salt and leave for 30 minutes to draw out the bitter juices. Rinse under cold, running water, drain and pat them dry with kitchen paper.

Stir the oil into the flour and gradually pour on the water, beating constantly. Season with salt. Stir in the beaten egg white just before using.

Heat the oil to 190C/375F. (At this temperature a 2.5-cm/1-in cube of day-old bread will turn golden brown in 50 seconds.) Spear the aubergine slices with a fork and dip them in the batter, allowing the excess to drip back into the bowl. Fry a few fritters at a time, for about 4 minutes, or until they are puffed up and golden. Drain them on kitchen paper and keep them warm while you fry the remainder.

To make the sauce, boil the lemon juice in a small pan until it is reduced to 30 ml/2 tbls. Add the butter a little at a time over very low heat, beating constantly. When all the butter has been added and the sauce is thick and creamy, stir in the chives and season with salt and pepper. To keep the sauce hot, stand in a larger pan of hot water and close-cover the surface with a piece of wetted greaseproof paper. Serve hot.

(You can cook mushroom fritters in the same way. Use 500 g/1 lb of medium-sized flat-cup mushrooms and trim the stalks to the caps.)

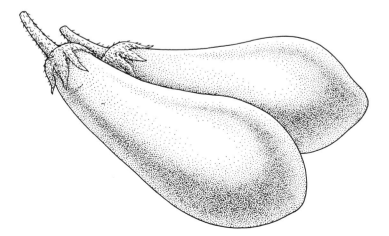

SHERRIED BRUSSELS SPROUTS

A popular "company" way to serve these small brassicas, as a tipsy accompaniment to meat dishes such as fried veal escallopes or grilled pork.

500 g/1 lb Brussels sprouts,
    trimmed
salt
25 g/1 oz butter
4 rashers bacon, rind
    removed, cut into cubes
30 ml/2 tbls flour
150 ml/¼ pt chicken stock
    (page 12)
90 ml/6 tbls medium sherry
150 ml/¼ pt soured cream
a large pinch of dried
    cinnamon
pepper
15 ml/1 tbls chopped parsley

Serves 4

Cook the Brussels sprouts in boiling, salted water for 10-12 minutes, until they are just tender. Drain, cool and slice in half lengthways.

Melt the butter, add the bacon and fry over moderate heat until crisp. Remove bacon and set aside. Stir in the flour, then gradually pour on the stock. Stir until the sauce boils and simmer for 2-3 minutes. Add the sherry, soured cream and cinnamon and season with salt and pepper. Allow just to heat through. Garnish with the bacon and parsley.

KANSAS CABBAGE

Creamed cabbage is a super accompaniment to hearty meat or game stews – in the early days in America's Midwest this would have been buffalo, deer, elk, rabbit or squirrel.

40 g/1½ oz butter
1 small cabbage
5 ml/1 tsp rock salt
pepper
a pinch of grated nutmeg
150 ml/¼ pt single cream
30 ml/2 tbls double cream

Serves 4-6

Melt the butter in a small flameproof casserole. Tear the cabbage into leaves and cut off any tough stalk. Turn it in the butter over moderate heat for 3-4 minutes. Sprinkle on the salt, pepper and nutmeg, pour on the single cream and stir gently. Cover and simmer over low heat for 5-7 minutes, until the cabbage is just tender. Taste and adjust seasoning if needed. Spoon the double cream over and serve at once.

DEEP-FRIED MUSHROOMS

Photograph opposite

Serve them as a first course with Hollandaise sauce or mayonnaise.

500 g/1 lb button mushrooms,
    trimmed
60 ml/4 tbls flour
salt and pepper
2 eggs
30 ml/2 tbls milk
75 g/3 oz breadcrumbs
25 g/1 oz grated Parmesan
    cheese
oil, for deep frying
2 lemons, to serve

Serves 6

Toss the mushrooms in the flour seasoned with salt and pepper. Mix together the egg and milk and stir in the mushrooms to coat them thoroughly. Put the breadcrumbs and cheese in a polythene bag and season with salt and pepper. Mix them by shaking the bag. Lift out the mushrooms with a draining spoon and toss them in the bag, a few at a time, in the crumb mixture. Heat the oil in a deep pan to 191C/380F and fry the mushrooms until they are golden brown. Drain them on kitchen paper and serve them at once, garnished with lemon wedges.

SOUTHERN CAROLINA OKRA PILAFF

Okra (or "ladies' fingers") was brought to the Southern States by Africans working on the rice plantations. Here it is teamed with long-grain Carolina rice in a pilaff which can be served with a simple salad, or to accompany spit-roast chicken.

6 rashers streaky bacon, rind
  removed, cut into small
  squares
2 medium onions, chopped
1 clove garlic, crushed
1 large green pepper, seeded
  and chopped
500 g/1 lb canned tomatoes
350 g/12 oz okra, topped and
  tailed and thinly sliced
250 g/8 oz long-grain Carolina
  rice
salt and pepper

Serves 6

Fry the bacon in a non-stick pan over moderate heat, stirring often, until it is crisp. Remove it with a draining spoon and set aside. Fry the onion and garlic in the fat in the pan and, when it is translucent, add the pepper. Fry, stirring, for 1 minute. Add the tomatoes and okra, bring to the boil, stir well, cover and simmer for 15 minutes.

Cook the rice in boiling, salted water for 12 minutes, or until it is just tender. Drain it into a colander, pour hot water through it and drain again. Stir the rice into the vegetable mixture, season with salt and pepper, cover and simmer over low heat for 10 minutes.

Remove from the heat and stand the pan in a warm place for 5 minutes. Garnish with the bacon.

PAN-FRIED CORN CAKES

Serve these small, golden, puffy little cakes with broiled chicken and banana, or steaks.

50 g/2 oz butter
1 small onion, finely chopped
25 g/1 oz flour
150 ml/¼ pt milk
200-g/7 -oz can corn niblets
salt and pepper
30 ml/2 tbls single cream
15 ml/1 tbls finely chopped
  chives, or green pepper
oil, for shallow frying

Serves 4-6

Melt the butter and fry the onion over moderate heat, stirring often, until it is translucent. Stir in the flour and when the mixture is thick gradually pour on the milk, stirring. Bring to the boil and simmer for 3 minutes.

Remove from the heat, beat in the corn and season with salt and pepper. Set aside to cool, then beat in the cream and chives or pepper. This mixture should be like a thick batter.

Heat a little oil in a heavy-based frying-pan and drop in 15 ml/1 tablespoon of the mixture. Fry over moderately high heat until the mixture sets and is brown on the underside. Flip over and fry the second side. Keep corn cakes warm while you fry the remainder. Serve very hot.

COURGETTE SOUFFLÉ

This high-rise soufflé of summer squash combined with Californian white wine makes an impressive, yet simple, first course or light main dish.

40 g/1½ oz butter
1 small onion, chopped
1 clove garlic, crushed
500 g/1 lb courgettes
  (zucchini), thinly sliced
150 ml/¼ pt sweet white wine
15 ml/1 tbls lemon juice
75 ml/5 tbls chicken stock
  (page 12)
salt and pepper
5 large eggs, separated
15 ml/1 tbls chopped summer
  savory, or parsley
45 ml/3 tbls grated Parmesan
  cheese

Serves 4-6

Melt the butter and fry the onion and garlic for 3-4 minutes over moderate heat, stirring once or twice. Add the courgettes and stir for 3 minutes. Pour on the wine, lemon juice and stock. Season with salt and pepper and bring to the boil. Simmer uncovered for 15 minutes, until the courgettes are tender but not collapsing. Turn into a bowl and set aside to cool.

Beat the egg yolks until thick and creamy, stir in the herb and cheese and stir into the courgette mixture. Beat the egg whites until stiff, then carefully fold them into the mixture. Pour into a greased 1.5-liter/2¾-pt soufflé dish.

Bake in the center of the oven at 200C/400F/gas 6 for 25-30 minutes, until the soufflé is well risen and has a golden crust on top. Serve at once.

(For a smooth texture, liquidize the vegetables in a blender or put them through a mouli-legumes before adding the liquids.)

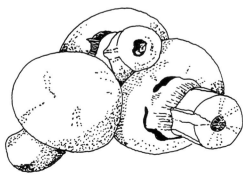
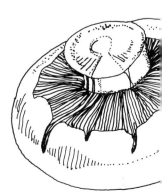

STUFFED CREAMED MUSHROOMS

Serve this adaptable and tasty dish as a first course, a savory to follow the meal, or as a snack, perhaps with slices of glazed ham.

20 large, flat mushrooms
50 g/2 oz butter
1 large onion, finely chopped
45 ml/3 tbls chopped parsley
45 ml/3 tbls sweet sherry
50 g/2 oz day-old white
    breadcrumbs
150 ml/¼ pt soured cream
salt and pepper
8 thin slices of bread, toasted

Serves 4

Cut off the mushroom stalks. Set aside the caps and chop the stalks. Melt the butter in a frying-pan and fry the onion for 3-4 minutes over moderate heat, stirring once or twice. Add the chopped mushroom stalks, parsley, sherry and breadcrumbs and stir well. Cook for 2 minutes. Remove from the heat, stir in the soured cream and season with salt and pepper.

Arrange the mushroom caps in a single layer in a shallow, well-greased baking dish. Divide the filling between them and press it well into the caps.

Cook in the oven at 200C/400F/gas 6 for 10-15 minutes, until the mushrooms are tender. Serve at once, on slices of toast, or garnished with toast triangles.

SWEET GLAZED ONIONS

Here's a simple dish that can be mostly prepared in advance, to accompany steaks, roast beef or golden chicken.

20 small onions
salt
50 g/2 oz butter
75 g/3 tbls soft light brown
    sugar
pepper
15 ml/1 tbls chopped parsley

Serves 4

Prick the peeled onions all over with a fork. Cook them in boiling, salted water for 10 minutes, then drain. Dry them thoroughly on kitchen paper.

Melt the butter, add the sugar and stir for 1 minute. Add the onions and stir constantly until they are glazed all over. Continue cooking over very low heat for 10 minutes, shaking occasionally, until the onions are caramelized. Serve at once. Garnish with the parsley.

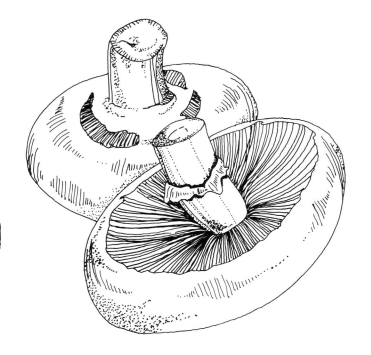

JERSEY PEPPER HASH

Tomatoes and green peppers, two abundant crops in the State of New Jersey, make a tasty side-dish to serve with broiled gammon and sunny-side-up fried eggs.

2 large green peppers, halved
    and seeded.
25 g/1 oz butter
2 medium onions, thinly
    sliced
350 g/12 oz tomatoes, skinned
    and chopped
5 ml/1 tsp sugar
salt and pepper
2 eggs, lightly beaten

Serves 4

Blanch the peppers in boiling water for 2 minutes. Drain them, pat dry with kitchen paper and thinly slice. Melt the butter and fry the onions over moderate heat for 3-4 minutes, stirring once or twice. Add the tomatoes and sugar, stir well and cook, uncovered, for 5 minutes. Add the peppers, season with salt and pepper, and cook for a further 10 minutes, until the peppers are tender. Taste, adjust seasoning if needed, stir in the eggs to scramble lightly in the hot vegetables, and serve at once.

MUSHROOM AND NUT PILAF

Photograph opposite

As a vegetarian main course or a meat accompaniment, a crunchy, colorful and glistening rice dish.

30 ml/2 tbls vegetable oil
250 g/8 oz brown short-grain
   rice
salt
1 medium onion, sliced
1 clove garlic, crushed
2 celery stalks, thinly sliced
1 green pepper, seeded and
   chopped
1 red pepper, seeded and
   chopped
75 g/3 oz cashew nuts
250 g/8 oz button
   mushrooms, quartered
pepper

Serves 4-6

Heat 15 ml/1 tbls of the oil in a large pan and stir in the rice. Cover with plenty of boiling, salted water, bring to the boil and cover the pan. Cook for 45 minutes. Drain.

   Meanwhile, heat the remaining oil in a pan and fry the onion, garlic and celery over moderate heat for 3 minutes, stirring once or twice. Add the peppers, cashews and mushrooms and cook over low heat, stirring occasionally, for 5 minutes.

   Stir in the cooked rice, season with salt and pepper and heat through gently. Serve hot.

SALAD NICOISE

This recipe from the south of France has been taken to the hearts of cooks all over the world, not forgetting America. Serve it as a main dish or starter.

250 g/8 oz frozen French
   beans, thawed
4 medium tomatoes, skinned
   and quartered
60 ml/4 tbls black olives
60 ml/4 tbls French dressing
   (page 92)
pepper
175 g/6 oz can tuna fish,
   drained and flaked
4 hard-boiled eggs, sliced in
   wedges

Serves 2 or 4

Toss together the beans, tomatoes, olives and dressing and season well with freshly ground black pepper. Very gently stir in the tuna fish. Turn into a serving bowl and arrange the egg slices on top.

GREEN GODDESS DRESSING

A mayonnaise sauce with chopped spring onions (scallions) and anchovies, this dressing is equally good with green salad or baked jacket potatoes.

200 ml/7 fl oz mayonnaise
   (page 96)
4 spring onions, thinly sliced
15 ml/1 tbls chopped parsley
5 ml/1 tsp chopped tarragon
15 ml/1 tbls tarragon vinegar
4 anchovy fillets, chopped
150 ml/¼ pt soured cream
pepper

Makes about 400 ml/14 fl oz

Gently beat all the ingredients together. Serve well chilled.

THOUSAND ISLAND DRESSING

This favorite Californian dressing is good with green salads of all kinds – lettuce, spinach, cucumber, watercress, Chinese leaves, thinly sliced avocados and courgettes. It's good as a topping for jacket potatoes, too.

200 ml/7 fl oz mayonnaise
   (page 96)
1 clove garlic, finely chopped
30 ml/2 tbls chopped pickled
   gherkins
45 ml/3 tbls tender celery
   heart, finely chopped
15 ml/1 tbls tomato purée
salt and cayenne pepper

Makes 300 ml/½ pt

Beat all the ingredients into the mayonnaise and season to taste with salt and cayenne. Serve well chilled.

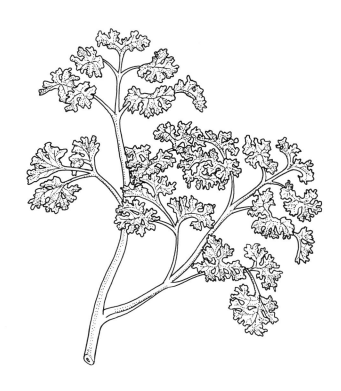

JACKET POTATOES WITH AVOCADO AND CHEESE DRESSING

A meal in themselves or a popular side dish, jacket-baked potatoes come in many guises. This one has a surprise dressing.

4 medium-large potatoes,
    scrubbed
1 small, ripe avocado, halved
    and stoned
5 ml/1 tsp lemon juice
100 g/4 oz Roquefort or other
    blue cheese
15 g/½ oz butter
salt and pepper

Serves 4

Prick the potatoes all over and bake them in the oven at 190C/375F/gas 5 for 1 hour, or until they are soft.

Split the potatoes in half and scoop out most of the flesh, leaving firm, unbroken "walls." Scoop the avocado flesh from the skin and add to the potato. Stir in the lemon juice, cheese and butter and season to taste with salt and pepper. Be sparing with the salt until you *have* tasted the mixture.

Mix well and pile the potato filling into the 8 half-shells. Place on a baking tray and return to the oven for 10 minutes. Serve very hot.

BRANDIED SWEET POTATOES

Sweet potatoes, a close relative of the native yams, are amazingly versatile, turning up as a handy vegetable accompaniment, an eye-catching highlight from Virginia, as here, and in desserts and baked goods (e.g. bread and cakes).

500 g/1 lb sweet potatoes,
    scrubbed
salt
50 g/2 oz butter
45 ml/3 tbls soft light-brown
    sugar
a pinch of ground cinnamon
45 ml/3 tbls brandy, warmed

Serves 4

Boil the potatoes in salted water for 20-25 minutes, until they are just tender. Drain, cool, peel and cut into 12-mm/½-in slices.

Heat the fat in a large, heavy-based frying-pan and fry the potatoes in a single layer over moderate heat for 4-5 minutes on each side. Turn them into a heated flameproof serving dish, sprinkle them with the sugar and cinnamon and pour on the brandy.

Light the spirit as you take the dish to the table, a triumph of blue flames.

PARSLEYED POTATOES

This is a good cook-ahead way of preparing a staple vegetable so that it can be quickly and gently reheated to serve with broiled steak or chicken.

45 ml/3 tbls vegetable oil
2 medium onions, chopped
2 cloves garlic, crushed
4 medium-large potatoes,
    peeled and cut into 6-mm/
    ¼-in slices
90 ml/6 tbls chopped parsley
300 ml/½ pt chicken stock
    (page 12), hot
salt and pepper
2 large, firm tomatoes, sliced

Serves 4

Heat the oil in a flameproof casserole and fry the onion and garlic over moderate heat for 3-4 minutes, stirring once or twice. Stir in the potato slices and turn them to coat them with oil. Sprinkle on the parsley, add the stock and season with salt and pepper. Bring to the boil and simmer for 10-15 minutes, until the potatoes are just tender, but in no danger of breaking. Garnish with the tomato slices.

To cook ahead, cook the potatoes for only 5 minutes. They will finish cooking as they are reheated.

WHOLESOME RICE SALAD

A corned beef hash with a difference – it's tossed with rice and peppers and served as part of a salad meal.

175 g/6 oz long-grain
    American rice
salt
75 ml/5 tbls soured cream
5 ml/1 tsp made mustard
pepper
250g/8 oz corned beef, diced
2 gherkins, chopped
1 red pepper, seeded and
    chopped
45 ml/3 tbls silver cocktail
    onions

Serves 4-6

Cook the rice in a large pan of boiling, salted water for 10 minutes, or until it is just tender. Drain and cool. Mix together the soured cream and mustard and season with salt and pepper.

Toss together the rice, corned beef, gherkins, red pepper and onions and stir in the soured cream dressing. Mix well.

GREEN SALAD

With barbecued steak, with hot-spiced chicken, poached salmon or fried eggs, green salad is the all-American accompaniment. Anything that's so simple must be prepared with extra care. Vary the ingredients according to seasonal availability.

1 medium lettuce – choose
    from Iceberg, Boston,
    Oakleaf, endive or escarole
175 g/6 oz Chinese cabbage,
    thinly sliced
1 bunch watercress sprigs
45 ml/3 tbls chopped fresh
    herbs, such as mint,
    parsley, chervil, thyme,
    chives, summer savory
10 ml/2 tsp olive oil
2.5 ml/½ tsp rock salt
French dressing
90 ml/6 tbls olive oil
30 ml/2 tbls white wine
    vinegar or cider vinegar
1 clove garlic, crushed
salt and pepper

Serves 6-8

Discard any damaged or tough outer leaves of the lettuce. Tear off the leaves, cut away any tough stalks and tear large leaves in half. Wash thoroughly and dry completely - a salad spinner is a must for salad buffs.

Toss the lettuce, Chinese leaves and watercress together, sprinkle on the oil and salt and toss well.

If the salad is to be stored before serving, pack it loosely into a large polythene bag and leave it in the bottom of the refrigerator – never leave it soaking in water. Toss it with oil and salt just before serving. Mix the dressing ingredients and pour over the salad on the point of serving. Toss well. For the best presentation, it is important to pre-chill the serving bowl and salad plates.

WILTED LETTUCE SALAD

The freshest, crispest lettuce leaves are needed to make this salad of sharp contrasts – the ice-cold greens and the piping hot dressing. Topped with chopped eggs and crumbled bacon, this salad from the American Mid-west makes a good light lunch or supper dish.

12 rashers streaky bacon, rind
    removed, cut into 2.5-cm/
    1-in cubes
2 medium lettuces, washed
    and thoroughly dried
16 medium radishes, thinly
    sliced
4 spring onions, thinly sliced
100 ml/3½ fl oz red wine
    vinegar
5 ml/1 tsp sugar
5 ml/1 tsp grated horseradish,
    or 10 ml/2 tsp creamed
    horseradish
1 small onion, finely chopped
salt and pepper
2 hard-boiled egg yolks,
    chopped

Serves 6

Fry the bacon in a non-stick pan over moderate heat for about 5 minutes, until it is crisp. Remove with a draining spoon and set aside. Toss together the lettuce, radishes and onions.

Stir the vinegar into the fat in the pan, add the sugar and horseradish and bring to the boil. Add the onion and cook for 2 minutes. Season with salt and pepper.

Immediately before serving, pour the hot dressing over the salad. Sprinkle on the bacon and then the egg.

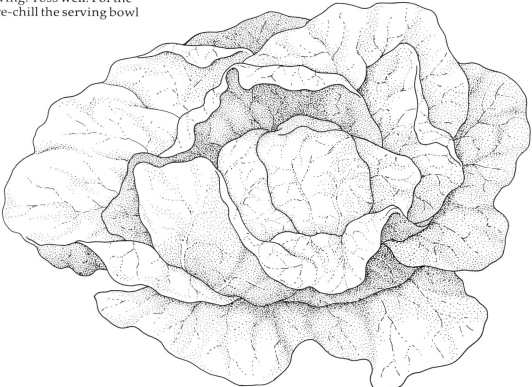

ASPARAGUS MOLDED SALAD

Good-to-look-at molded salads are an appetizing feature of American buffet tables. This one, combining whole asparagus spears and chopped carrots in a creamy setting, perfectly fits the bill.

250 g/8 oz packet frozen
   asparagus spears
250 g/8 oz carrots, finely diced
salt
10 ml/2 tsp aspic jelly crystals
300 ml/½ pt chicken stock
   (page 12)
15 g/½ oz powdered gelatine
25 g/1 oz sugar
15 ml/1 tbls mustard powder
3 eggs, lightly beaten
90 ml/6 tbls white wine
   vinegar
300 ml/½ pt single cream
pepper
1 bunch watercress sprigs

Serves 6

Cook the asparagus and carrots separately in boiling, salted water until they are just tender. Drain them and pat them dry with kitchen paper. Leave to cool.

Mix the aspic jelly crystals with the chicken stock, following the directions on the packet. When the aspic becomes syrupy, like unbeaten egg whites, pour it into an 850-ml/1½-pt decorative mold and twist and turn it until the jelly coats the surface. Arrange the asparagus evenly around the mold, the tops to the centre. Set aside in the refrigerator.

Sprinkle the gelatine on 45 ml/3 tbls water in a small bowl, stir and stand in a pan of hot water for about 5 minutes, to soften. Mix together the sugar, mustard and eggs. Boil the vinegar in a small pan, tip in the egg mixture and stir over very low heat until it thickens. Remove from the heat. Stir in the gelatine and leave to cool.

When the egg mixture begins to thicken, stir in the cream and carrots and season with salt and pepper. Pour slowly into the mold. Chill in the refrigerator for at least 3 hours to set. Turn out on to a plate and garnish the edge with watercress sprigs.

CAULIFLOWER AND BACON SALAD

Photograph on page 82

1 large cauliflower
salt
15 ml/1 tbls lemon juice
8 rashers streaky bacon
30 ml/2 tbls capers
45 g/1¾ oz can anchovy fillets,
   drained and chopped
50 g/2 oz black olives
30 ml/2 tbls chopped chives
Dressing
90 ml/6 tbls vegetable oil
30 ml/2 tbls red wine vinegar
5 ml/1 tsp made mustard
1 clove garlic, crushed

Serves 6

Cut the leaves and stalk from the cauliflower (you can use them for soup) and cut into florets. Cook in boiling water with salt and lemon juice for 4 minutes. Drain.

Meanwhile, mix together the dressing ingredients. Toss the hot cauliflower in the dressing and leave to cool.

Grill the bacon until crisp and cut it into squares. Just before serving, toss it with the cauliflower, capers, anchovies, olives and chives.

VEGETARIAN PASTA SALAD

Photograph opposite

A combination of corn, pasta and crunchy vegetables, this salad can be served as a light meal or as an accompaniment to cold meats and cheeses.

350 g/12 oz pasta spirals (or
   other shapes)
salt
60 ml/4 tbls French dressing
   (page 92)
4 stalks young celery, thinly
   sliced
1 red pepper, seeded and
   chopped
350g/12 oz can sweetcorn
   kernels, drained
6 spring onions, chopped
100 g/4 oz button
   mushrooms, thinly sliced

Serves 6

Cook the pasta in a large pan of boiling, salted water for 10 minutes, or according to the directions on the packet. Drain, refresh in cold water and drain again thoroughly. Toss with the dressing and leave to cool.

Toss in the celery, pepper, sweetcorn and onions and mix well.

Make a ring of mushroom slices around a serving dish and spoon the salad into the center.

SPINACH SALAD

This cool, crisp salad of the youngest spinach leaves is worthy of a course to itself.

1 medium cucumber, peeled,
   seeded and finely diced
salt
250 g/8 oz young, tender
   spinach leaves, washed and
   dried
1 young celery heart, thinly
   sliced
60 ml/4 tbls pine nuts
Dressing
75 ml/5 tbls olive oil
15 ml/1 tbls white wine
   vinegar
15 ml/1 tbls lemon juice
pepper
1 small onion, finely chopped
4 small cocktail gherkins,
   finely chopped
15 ml/1 tbls chopped parsley
2 hard-boiled eggs, chopped

Serves 4

Put the cucumber into a colander over a bowl, sprinkle with salt and leave for 30 minutes. Tear the stalks from the spinach leaves and tear the leaves in half. Rinse the cucumber under cold running water, drain and pat dry with kitchen paper. In the serving bowl, toss together the cucumber, spinach, celery and pine nuts. Mix the oil, vinegar and lemon juice, season with salt and pepper and stir in the onion, gherkins and parsley. Just before serving, pour the dressing over the salad and toss thoroughly. Sprinkle the chopped egg to garnish.

CAESAR SALAD

This salad is thought to have originated in the 1920's in Southern California, though the inclusion of Parmesan cheese points to Italian heritage. The main feature is the combination of crisp green leaves and crunchy fried garlic croûtons.

about 75 ml/5 tbls vegetable
   oil
4 × 2.5-cm/1-in thick slices
   white bread, cut into cubes
3 cloves garlic, finely chopped
2 medium Cos lettuces,
   washed, dried and chilled
50 g/2 oz can anchovy fillets,
   drained and chopped
1 small onion, finely chopped
125 g/4 oz grated Parmesan
   cheese
Dressing
90 ml/6 tbls olive oil
30 ml/2 tbls red wine vinegar
5 ml/1 tsp lemon juice
5 ml/1 tsp mustard powder
2.5 ml/½ tsp sugar
salt and pepper
1 egg, lightly beaten

Serves 6-8

Heat the oil in a frying-pan and fry the bread cubes over moderate heat for 5-6 minutes, stirring often, until they are deep golden brown. Add a little more oil if necessary. Toss the croûtons on kitchen paper to dry, then stir them with the garlic.

Tear the lettuce leaves into pieces and put them in a chilled bowl.

Mix together the dressing ingredients, stirring in the egg when the others are well blended. Pour over the lettuce just before serving and toss well. Add the anchovy, onion and cheese, toss thoroughly and scatter on the croûtons. Serve on chilled plates.

WALDORF SALAD

Photograph on pages 98-99

One of America's own culinary innovations which must be served well chilled and absolutely fresh.

6 dessert apples, cored and
    cubed
30 ml/2 tbls lemon juice
150 g/5 oz walnuts, roughly
    chopped
2 tender celery hearts, thinly
    sliced
lettuce leaves, to serve
Mayonnaise
2 egg yolks
30 ml/2 tbls white wine
    vinegar
15 ml/1 tbls French mustard
120 ml/8 tbls olive oil
salt and pepper

Serves 6

Toss the apples at once in the lemon juice to preserve their color and toss with the walnuts and celery. Line a serving plate with lettuce leaves.

To make the mayonnaise (which can be done well in advance) beat together the egg yolks, vinegar and mustard and gradually pour on the oil drop by drop, beating all the time, until the sauce is thick and glossy. Season with salt and pepper.

Toss the salad with the mayonnaise at the point of serving and pile it on the bed of lettuce.

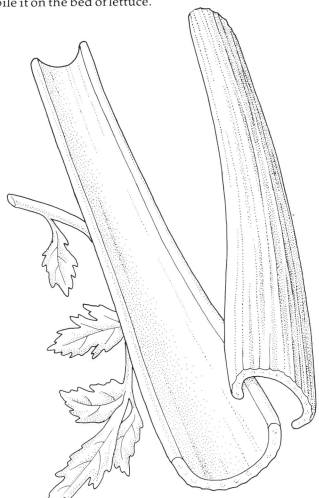

NEW ENGLAND COLESLAW

The boiled soured cream dressing and the caraway seeds are the characteristics of this much-plagiarized cabbage salad.

1 small, firm white cabbage,
    coarsely shredded
3 large carrots, grated
1 medium onion, grated
5 ml/1 tsp caraway seeds
Dressing
40 g/1½ oz butter
25 g/1 oz flour
10 ml/2 tsp mustard powder
10 ml/2 tsp sugar
75 ml/5 tbls white distilled
    vinegar
5 ml/1 tsp lemon juice
150 ml/¼ pt milk
2 eggs, lightly beaten
150 ml/¼ pt soured cream
salt and pepper

Serves 8

Soak the cabbage in iced water in the refrigerator for 2 hours. Drain and dry thoroughly – using a salad spinner is infinitely quicker and more efficient than any other means. Mix with the carrot, onion and caraway.

Melt the butter in a pan, stir in the flour and mustard powder, then the sugar and vinegar to make a smooth paste. Stir in the lemon juice, milk and eggs and beat over low heat for about 10 minutes, or until the mixture thickens. Beat in the soured cream, season with salt and pepper and leave to cool. Pour over the salad and toss well.

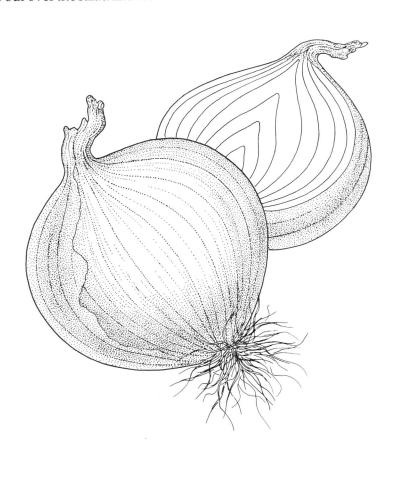

AVOCADO WITH PEANUT DRESSING

Two great crops of the American continent come together for a first course with good texture and flavor contrasts.

2 large, ripe avocados
60 ml/4 tbls olive oil
30 ml/2 tbls cider vinegar
5 ml/1 tsp caster sugar
2.5 ml/½ tsp mustard powder
pepper
a pinch of ground mace
60 ml/4 tbls salted peanuts,
　chopped
30 ml/2 tbls stuffed green
　olives, sliced

Serves 4

Mix together the oil, vinegar, sugar, mustard, pepper and mace and stir in the peanuts and olives. Just before serving, halve and stone the avocados and pour on the dressing.

POTATO SALAD

Many potato salad recipes popular in America owe their origins to the German settlers. This one is best served warm, with pork or veal dishes or to accompany baked ham.

500 g/1 lb small potatoes,
　scrubbed
salt
4 thick rashers streaky bacon,
　rind removed, and cut in
　squares
10 ml/2 tsp sugar
15 ml/1 tbls flour
75 ml/5 tbls cider vinegar
pepper
6 celery stalks, thinly sliced
3 spring onions, chopped
1 green pepper, seeded and
　chopped

Serves 4

Cook the potatoes in boiling water until they are just tender. Drain them, cool slightly, rub off the skins and halve. Fry the bacon in a non-stick pan for 5 minutes over moderate heat, stirring often, then remove with a draining spoon. Stir the sugar and flour into the fat in the pan, pour on 60 ml/4 tbls water and stir to a smooth paste. Add the vinegar, stirring constantly. Simmer for 5 minutes and season with salt and pepper.

　In a serving bowl, toss together the potatoes, bacon, celery, chopped onion and green pepper. Pour over the dressing, toss well and serve warm, if possible.

RICE SALAD

At any "bring a dish" party, you can bet someone's sure to bring a super rice salad.

2 red and 2 green peppers,
　seeded and halved
　lengthways
250 g/8 oz French beans,
　topped and tailed
salt
500 g/1 lb firm tomatoes,
　thinly sliced
125 g/4 oz green grapes,
　skinned and seeded
125 g/4 oz black olives, halved
　and stoned
125 g/4 oz pecan halves
125 g/4 oz seedless raisins
175 g/6 oz cooked long-grain
　rice
Dressing
150 ml/¼ pt soured cream
30 ml/2 tbls olive oil
10 ml/2 tsp orange juice
5 ml/1 tsp grated orange rind
pepper

Serves 6

Broil the pepper halves skin side up under a hot grill for 7 minutes, or until the skin blackens. Peel off the skin and cut the flesh into 2.5-cm/1-in squares. Cook the beans in boiling, salted water until they are just tender. Drain, cool and cut into 2.5-cm/1-in lengths. In a serving bowl, toss the peppers and beans with all the other salad ingredients.

　Mix the soured cream, oil, orange juice and rind and season with salt and pepper. Pour over the rice salad and toss well.

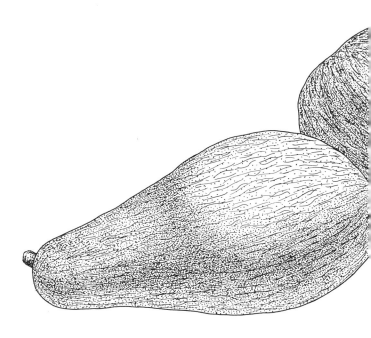

PINTO BEAN SALAD

In America's Southwest states of Arizona, New Mexico, Oklahoma and Texas, the pinto bean reigns supreme. This salad may be served as part of a buffet, as a first course or a side dish.

250 g/8 oz dried pinto beans,
   soaked overnight and
   drained
175 g/6 oz mild cheese, diced
1 large Spanish onion, thinly
   sliced
lettuce leaves to serve
2 hard-boiled eggs, chopped
1 canned pimento, drained
   and thinly sliced
Dressing
60 ml/4 tbls peanut oil
20 ml/4 tsp red wine vinegar
a pinch of sugar
salt and pepper

Serves 6

Cook the beans in boiling, unsalted water for 1 hour, or until they are tender. Drain them and rinse under hot water. Drain again thoroughly.
   Mix together the dressing ingredients and pour over the hot beans. Leave to cool. Toss in the cheese and onion. Line a dish with lettuce leaves, pile on the salad and sprinkle with the chopped egg. Garnish with a lattice pattern of pimento strips.

GUACAMOLE

This Latin American dish has been adopted throughout the United States as a dip, spread and filling for bouchées or celery boats. In fact, it is the perfect party snack. Choose the Californian Hass avocados, with their black, knobbly skins and rich flavor. They are available from April to September.

2 ripe avocados
45 ml/3 tbls lemon juice
10 ml/2 tsp olive oil
1 clove garlic, crushed
1 small onion, finely chopped
45 ml/3 tbls chopped celery
   leaves
½ small red pepper, seeded
   and finely chopped
salt and pepper
a pinch of cayenne pepper

Serves 6

Peel and stone the avocados and mash the flesh with the lemon juice. Beat in the remaining ingredients, taste and adjust seasoning if needed.
   Since avocados tend to discolor quickly, make the spread as close as possible to serving. For quickness, have the remaining ingredients mixed ready, and add the avocado last. If you have to store, keep in a covered container in the refrigerator for up to 12 hours.

AVOCADO RING

From America's West Coast, a creamy ring that is delicious filled with prawns, chopped crab meat or a crispy apple salad.

300 ml/½ pt chicken stock
   (page 12)
20 ml/4 tsp powdered gelatine
2 large, ripe avocados, halved,
   stoned and peeled
150 ml/¼ pt soured cream
15 ml/1 tbls lemon juice
a pinch of cayenne pepper
salt and pepper
1 large cucumber, very thinly
   sliced

Serves 6

Put 60 ml/4 tbls of the stock in a small bowl, sprinkle on the gelatine, stir well and stand in a bowl of hot water for about 15 minutes. Boil the remaining stock, pour on the gelatine mixture and set aside to cool – pour it into a bowl and stand in iced water to save time.
   Liquidize the avocado flesh with a little of the stock, or press it through a sieve. When the stock is beginning to set, stir it gradually into the avocado, beat in the cream and lemon juice and season with cayenne, salt and pepper.
   Pour the mixture into a wetted 850-ml/1½-pt ring mold and leave in the refrigerator for at least 2 hours to set.
   Turn it onto a plate and surround the edge with cucumber slices. Fill the center with a salad of your choice.
   (As an alternative, use 350 g/12 oz tomatoes, skinned and liquidized or sieved, in place of the avocado. Season with a few drops of Worcestershire sauce.)

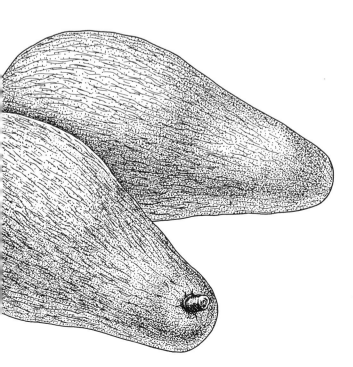

6: DESSERTS

In spite of the prime meat, the fresh fish and the succulent vegetables she produces, America is probably most loved by gourmets for her desserts. From the 17th century, when housewives used to snip a corner off the blue paper cone of sugar, to the present day, when many try to cut down on sweeteners, America's meals have always ended with a triumphant flourish.

There has never been a shortage of grains and the earliest puddings, owing their origins to the Indians, were humble but tasty boiled or baked affairs made with cornmeal, dried fruits and spices. Some were little more than unleavened bread sweetened with maple. But as all Vermonters will testify, if you love maple sugar or syrup, it doesn't much matter what goes with it. Waffles, pancakes, fritters, custards or ice cream are all the more delicious for this sticky sap of the maple tree.

Ice cream is America's top favorite dessert, and has never looked back since it was introduced from Europe in the 18th century. Thomas Jefferson wrote out a recipe for it, using 6 egg yolks and 2 pints of heavy cream, and George Washington's household purchased "a cream machine for ice" so that it could be served at the top tables. As a vehicle for fruit and other flavorings, not to mention colorings, ice cream and its close relative, the sorbet, are hard to surpass. As a spectacular ending to a meal, baked Alaska – the meringue surprise developed at Delmonico's restaurant in New York - goes unrivaled in American circles.

After ice cream in the popularity poll comes the pie, with apple pie way ahead of others. *Real* apple pie, which we have elevated to the "Highdays and Holidays" section (page 78), has two crusts. In Maine, custom dictates that it is splashed with cold water before baking, to give the pastry extra flakiness – a tip worth trying. Pennsylvania Dutch shoo-fly pie, sticky with molasses and spiced with cloves; lemon chiffon pie; pecan pie; raisin and soured cream pie and a less calorie-laden grapefruit pie, both with vinegar shortcrust pastry – you can travel across time and the States with mouthwatering pastry recipes.

A very special kind of pie, cheesecake, came to America with the immigrants from Eastern Europe, although some say it was there, in other forms, already. Our recipe for baked New York cheesecake is as different from strawberry jello cheesecake as, well, chalk from cheese, and there are peach and apple versions in between.

Fruit has always been plentiful in America. The Settlers found wild blackberries, blueberries, raspberries, cranberries, plums and cherries. Blueberry grunt and plum custard are two ways they used them.

Nowadays many other fruits are cultivated from coast to coast, and the State promotion boards compete with each other for variety, succulence and the world markets. Red Delicious apples which enjoy an eleven-month season, the Bing variety of cherries which are harvested in July and August and slot in neatly after the European crops are over, Red Emperor dessert grapes, Hass avocados with their distinctive black and knobbly skins, oranges, lemons and limes, pears, peaches and pineapples – America is one great big basket of delicious and health-giving fruits.

GRAPEFRUIT PIE

Vinegar shortcrust pastry is topped with golden grapefruit segments in this sweet-and-sour dessert speciality from Arizona.

Vinegar shortcrust pastry
225 g/7 oz flour
a pinch of salt
5 ml/1 tsp sugar
75 g/3 oz lard
1 small egg
5 ml/1 tsp white distilled
  vinegar
Filling
50 g/2 oz flour
175 g/6 oz soft light brown
  sugar
a pinch of salt
2 large eggs
300 ml/½ pt single cream,
  heated
125 ml/4 fl oz unsweetened
  grapefruit juice
2 large grapefruit
5 ml/1 tsp vanilla essence

Serves 6

To make the pastry, sift the flour, salt and sugar together, cut the lard in small pieces and rub in until the mixture resembles fine breadcrumbs. Beat the egg with 20 ml/4 tsp iced water and the vinegar. Gradually pour the liquid on to the dry ingredients, stirring constantly. Form into a dough.

Roll out the dough on a lightly-floured board, line a greased 25-cm/10-in flan case and trim the edges. Bake "blind" in the oven at 190C/375F/gas 5 for 25 minutes. Set aside to cool.

To make the filling, put the flour, 150 g/5 oz of the sugar and the salt in the top of a double boiler or a bowl fitted over a pan of hot water. Stir in the eggs and cream and stir over simmering water for about 20 minutes, or until the custard thickens. Stir in the grapefruit juice, 10 ml/2 tsp grated grapefruit rind and the vanilla essence and cook for a further 5 minutes, stirring occasionally. Remove from the heat.

Separate the grapefruit into segments and remove the pips. Pour the hot custard into the baked pie case and arrange the grapefruit segments in a wheel pattern. Sprinkle the remaining sugar over the fruit and brown under a hot grill. Serve warm or chilled.

RAISIN AND SOURED CREAM PIE

Recipes using soured cream were brought to the American Mid-west in the early 19th century by Eastern European immigrants.

25-cm/10-in unbaked
  vinegar-crust flan case
225 g/7 oz sugar
2 large eggs
300 ml/½ pt soured cream
5 ml/1 tsp white distilled
  vinegar
a pinch of salt
2.5 ml/½ tsp ground
  cinnamon
2.5 ml/½ tsp ground allspice
175 g/6 oz seedless raisins

Serves 6

Partly bake the flan case in the oven at 200C/400F/gas 6 for 10 minutes.

Beat the sugar, eggs and soured cream until thick, stir in the vinegar, salt and spices and stir in the raisins. Pour the filling into the flan case and bake for 30-35 minutes, or until the custard is set and the top is golden brown. Serve warm or chilled.

LEMON CHIFFON PIE

Snowy-white, high-rise and light as a feather, a tangy dessert that is always impressive.

22.5-cm/9-in baked
  shortcrust flan case (page
  105)
3 lemons
4 eggs
175 g/6 oz caster sugar
15 ml/1 tbls powdered
  gelatine
150 ml/¼ pt double cream,
  whipped

Serves 6-8

Grate the rind of 1 lemon and thinly pare the rind of another. Cut the rind into very thin matchstick strips. Squeeze the juice of all 3 lemons. Put the strips of peel into a small pan, cover with boiling water and simmer for 15 minutes. Drain and pat dry.

Put the egg yolks, 125 g/4 oz sugar, gelatine and 150 ml/¼ pt water into the top of a double boiler or a bowl fitted over a pan of simmering water. Stir for about 15-20 minutes until the mixture thickens. Stir in the lemon juice and grated rind. Stand the pan or bowl in cold water and chill for about 20 minutes, until the mixture starts to thicken.

Stir in most of the cream, reserving a little for decoration. Stiffly whisk the egg whites, fold in the remaining sugar and fold the meringue mixture into the lemon mixture.

Pour it into the flan case and swirl the top. Pipe rosettes of cream to decorate and scatter with the lemon strips. Serve chilled.

SHOO-FLY PIE

This ultra-sweet flan has layers of molasses and spiced crumbs which make a sticky-toffee filling on a bed of raisins.

Shortcrust pastry
150 g/5 oz flour
a pinch of salt
125 g/4 oz white vegetable fat
Filling
175 g/6 oz seedless raisins
125 g/4 oz molasses sugar
125 g/4 oz molasses
45 ml/3 tbls orange juice
2.5 ml/½ tsp bicarbonate of soda
2 eggs, beaten
175 g/6 oz wholewheat flour
2.5 ml/½ tsp ground ginger
5 ml/1 tsp ground cinnamon
a pinch of grated nutmeg
a pinch of ground cloves
50 g/2 oz butter
50 g/2 oz mixed candied peel, very finely chopped

Serves 8

To make the pastry, sift together the flour and salt and rub in the fat until the mixture resembles fine breadcrumbs. Mix to a dough with a little iced water. Roll out the dough on a lightly-floured board, line a 25-cm/10-in flan ring and trim the edges. Spread the raisins over the pastry and set aside. Put the sugar and molasses into a small bowl, stir in the orange juice and 75 ml/5 tbls boiling water and beat well. Stir in the soda and eggs and beat until all the ingredients are well blended.

Mix together the wholewheat flour and spices and rub in the butter until the mixture resembles fine crumbs. Stir in the peel. Spoon half the molasses mixture over the raisins, then half the crumbs. Repeat the layers. Bake in the oven at 200C/400F/gas 6 for 15 minutes. Lower the heat to 180C/350F/gas 4 and cook for a further 20-25 minutes, or until the top layer forms a firm crust. Serve warm, with whipped soured cream.

PECAN PIE

A very rich, wickedly fattening and quite irresistible traditional American dessert.

22.5-cm/9-in unbaked shortcrust flan case
4 eggs
350 g/12 oz golden syrup
50 g/2 oz soft light brown sugar
a pinch of salt
25 g/1 oz butter, melted
5 ml/1 tsp vanilla essence
60 ml/4 tbls double cream
175 g/6 oz shelled pecans

Serve 6-8

Beat the eggs, syrup, sugar and salt and stir in the melted butter, vanilla and cream. Chop 150g/5 oz of the nuts and stir them into the mixture. Pour the filling into the flan case and arrange the remaining nuts on top.

Bake in the oven at 200C/400F/gas 6 for 10 minutes. Reduce heat to 180C/350F/gas 4 and continue cooking for a further 30-35 minutes, until the filling is set. Cover the top with foil if the nuts brown too quickly. Serve cold, with single or double cream.

NEW ORLEANS BANANAS

Headily spiced and flamed with rum, this is a quick and exciting way to serve bananas.

50 g/2 oz unsalted butter
50 g/2 oz soft dark brown sugar
a pinch of grated nutmeg
1.5 ml/¼ tsp ground allspice
150 ml/¼ pt dark rum (or crème de cacao)
4 medium, ripe bananas, peeled and halved lengthways
50 g/2 oz pecan halves
vanilla ice cream, to serve

Serves 4

Melt the butter in a frying pan over low heat, stir in the sugar, nutmeg and allspice and half the rum and stir until the sugar has dissolved. Add the banana halves and pecans, bring the sauce to the boil and simmer for 5 minutes, basting the fruit with the sauce once or twice.

Heat the remaining rum. Transfer the fruit to a heated serving dish. Pour all but 30 ml/2 tbls of the rum over the bananas and light it. Serve at once while the blue flames are at their most spectacular. Serve the ice cream separately, with the remaining rum poured over.

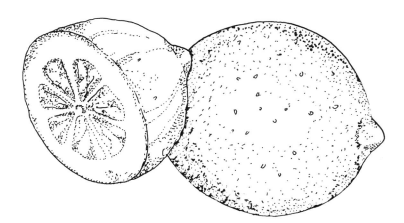

108

BLUEBERRY GRUNT

A steamed pudding from New England, featuring the deliciously tart wild blueberries of the region. Blackberries can be used instead.

75 ml/5 tbls clear honey
750 g/1 ½ lb fresh or frozen
  and thawed blueberries, or
  blackberries
375 g/12 oz flour
125 g/4 oz caster sugar
15 ml/1 tbls baking powder
2.5 ml/½ tsp ground
  cinnamon
40 g/1½ oz butter
125 ml/4 fl oz milk

Serves 6

Grease a 1.75-liter/3-pt pudding basin, put the honey in the bottom and add the fruit. Sift together the flour, sugar, baking powder and cinnamon and rub in the butter. Pour on the milk and stir to form a soft batter. Spread over the fruit and level the top.

Cover the basin with greased greaseproof paper and with a piece of greased white cotton or foil and tie securely. Stand on a trivet in a large pan of boiling water and steam for 1 ¾ hours, topping up with more boiling water as needed. Turn out onto a heated serving dish. Serve hot with cream or custard.

INDIAN PUDDING

This baked spiced custard is thickened with cornmeal, the "flour" of the American Indians.

125 g/4 oz seedless raisins
60 ml/4 tbls dark rum
600 ml/1 pt milk
50 g/2 oz fine cornmeal
a pinch of salt
40 g/1½ oz butter
2 large eggs, lightly beaten
60 ml/4 tbls sugar
5 ml/1 tsp ground allspice
1.5 ml/¼ tsp ground
  cinnamon
a pinch of ground cloves

Serves 6

Soak the raisins in the rum. Scald the milk and beat in the cornmeal and salt. Stir over very low heat until the custard thickens, stir in the butter and remove from the heat. Leave to cool for about 10 minutes.

Beat in the eggs, sugar and spices and stir in the raisins. Pour into an ovenproof dish standing in a roasting pan half filled with hot water. Bake in the oven at 150C/300F/gas 2 for 1-1 ¼ hours, or until the custard is set and golden brown on top. Serve warm, with whipped cream.

ICED LEMON PUDDING

The great advantage of this refreshingly zingy pudding is that you don't have to remember to take it out of the freezer in advance – you serve it frozen.

175 g/6 oz butter, softened
200 g/7 oz caster sugar
3 eggs, separated
grated rind and juice of 2
  lemons
30 ml/2 tbls orange liqueur
18 sponge fingers

Serves 8

Beat the butter and 175 g/6 oz of the sugar until light and fluffy. Beat in the egg yolks one at a time, then the lemon rind and juice and the liqueur. Whisk the egg whites until they are stiff, fold in the remaining sugar and fold the meringue into the lemon mixture.

Line a 500-g/1-lb loaf tin with foil. Make a layer of sponge, spoon on a layer of the lemon mixture and repeat the layers, finishing with lemon. Wrap in foil and freeze for at least 3 hours.

COFFEE AND RUM BAVAROIS

Photograph on page 106

A light, creamy dessert that is a perfect dinner party choice.

600 ml/1 pt milk
60 ml/4 tbls coffee granules
4 large eggs, separated
5 ml/1 tsp cornflour
  (cornstarch)
125 g/4 oz caster sugar
15 ml/1 tbls powdered
  gelatine
75 ml/5 tbls dark rum
150 ml/¼ pt double cream,
  whipped

Serves 6

Heat the milk to just below boiling point and stir in the coffee. Set aside for 10 minutes. Beat the egg yolks with the cornflour and half the sugar until thick. Gradually strain on the milk, beating constantly. Turn into the top of a double boiler or a bowl fitted over a pan of simmering water. Stir for about 15 minutes, or until the custard thickens.

Soften the gelatine in 45 ml/3 tbls hot water. Gradually pour the gelatine and the rum into the custard, blending it in thoroughly, and set aside to cool.

Whisk the egg whites until stiff and fold in the remaining sugar. Fold into the custard, then fold in most of the cream, reserving a little to decorate. Chill in the refrigerator for about 3 hours, to set. Decorate the top with piped rosettes of cream.

CREME BRULEE

Cream from the home farm was never made into a more delicious dessert than this. It is specially good with fruit salad or frosted fruits.

4 egg yolks
75 g/3 oz caster sugar
300 ml/½ pt double cream
300 ml/½ pt milk
1 vanilla pod

Serves 6

Beat the egg yolks with 15 ml/1 tbls of the sugar. Heat the cream and milk with the vanilla pod. Strain onto the egg mixture and pour into the top of a double boiler or a pan fitted over a pan of simmering water. Stir for about 20 minutes, or until the custard thickens enough to coat the back of a spoon. Strain the custard into a flameproof dish and set aside to cool for at least 2 hours. Wash and dry the vanilla pod for future use.

Sprinkle the remaining sugar evenly over the surface and caramellize under a hot grill. Cool before serving.

KIWI FRUIT SURPRISE

Photograph p 107

You can whip it up in moments and leave it in the refrigerator all day. The result is magic!

200 ml/7 fl oz double cream
300 ml/11 fl oz plain yoghurt
150 g/5 oz light Muscovado
  sugar
4 kiwi fruits, peeled and
  sliced crosswise
100 g/4 oz fresh strawberries,
  hulled and sliced

Serves 6

Whip the cream until it is almost stiff, then fold into the yoghurt. Turn into small individual serving dishes. Sprinkle the sugar evenly on top and chill in the refrigerator for at least 24 hours. The sugar seeps slowly through the cream mixture, making sweet ripples.

Arrange the fruit slices on top just before serving.

PINEAPPLE ALASKAS

Individual desserts with an exciting center, specially popular with children.

3 egg whites
125 g/4 oz caster sugar
75 g/2 oz desiccated coconut
6 slices fresh or canned and
  drained pineapple
1 block of bought or home-
  made vanilla ice cream
a few strips of candied
  angelica

Serves 6

Whisk the egg whites until stiff, add half the sugar and whisk again until the meringue holds stiff peaks. Fold in the remaining sugar and all but 30 ml/2 tbls of the desiccated coconut.

Place a piece of pineapple on each of 6 heatproof plates and pile ice cream in a high mound on each one. Cover completely with meringue and sprinkle with the remaining coconut. Bake in the oven at 220C/425F/gas 7 for 3 minutes.

Arrange the angelica in the meringue tops to represent fronds and serve at once.

WAFFLES WITH SOURED CREAM AND BLUEBERRIES

Photograph on page 115
Waffles are wonderful for breakfast, snacks or desserts, with maple syrup, honey or fruit.

250 g/8 oz self-raising flour
2.5 ml/½ tsp salt
5 ml/1 tsp baking powder
2 eggs
75 g/3 oz butter, melted
400 ml/¾ pt buttermilk
475 g/15 oz can blueberry pie
   filling
300 ml/½ pt soured cream, to
   serve

Serves 6

Sift together the flour, salt and baking powder and beat in the eggs and melted butter. Gradually pour on the buttermilk, beating all the time. Beat until smooth.
   Heat the waffle iron, pour in the batter, cover and cook according to the instructions for your appliance. Keep the first batch of waffles warm while you cook the remainder.
   Heat the pie filling. Sandwich the waffles together in pairs with the blueberry mixture and serve with the soured cream.

BAKED ALASKA

Photograph opposite

Versions of this magic dessert with the surprise center are served in restaurants very far removed from Alaska.

3 egg whites
175 g/6 oz caster sugar
20-cm/8-in sponge cake
1 block of bought or home-
   made vanilla ice cream

Serves 6

Whisk the egg whites until they are stiff. Add half the sugar and whisk again until the meringue stands in stiff peaks. Fold in the remaining sugar.
   Stand the sponge cake on a heatproof dish and cover it with the ice cream. Spread the meringue over to cover the ice cream completely at the top and sides. Bake in the oven at 220C/425F/gas 7 for 3 minutes. Serve at once.

MERINGUE ICE CREAM

This is *the* perfect ice cream to serve with the season's choicest soft fruits.

175 g/6 oz meringues,
    crushed
10 ml/2 tsp grated lemon rind
450 ml/¾ pt double cream,
    whipped

Serves 6

Stir the meringues and lemon rind into the cream. Turn the mixture into a 500-g/1-lb loaf tin lined with foil. Cover and freeze (without the need for whisking) for 3 hours. Leave in the main part of the refrigerator for 30 minutes before serving.

PRALINE

Praline is a good dessert stand-by. Serve it lightly crushed or finely powdered to top fruit creams, mousses and ice cream, as a quickie-pud on banana halves or stirred into whipped cream with a dash of liqueur.

175 g/6 oz sugar
175 g/6 oz blanched almonds

Put the sugar and 75 ml/5 tbls water into a pan and dissolve over low heat, stirring. Increase the heat and, without stirring again, heat the sugar until it turns caramel brown. Add the almonds and stir with a wooden spoon.
    Turn the mixture onto a greased jelly roll pan (Swiss roll tin) and leave to cool. Break into pieces and crush with a rolling pin or reduce to powder in a blender. Store in an airtight tin.

BLUEBERRY SORBET

Decorate chilled and frosted glasses of this richly colored sorbet with scented geranium leaves for a memorable meal ending.

175 g/6 oz sugar
1 kg/2¼ lb fresh or frozen and
    thawed blueberries
juice of 2 lemons
2 egg whites, stiffly beaten
30 ml/2 tbls kirsch (optional),
    to serve

Serves 6

Put the sugar in a pan with 300 ml/½ pt water and stir over low heat to dissolve. Increase the heat and boil for 10 minutes. Set aside to cool. Purée the blueberries in a blender, or press them through a nylon sieve. Stir in the lemon juice and syrup.
    Turn the mixture into two 600-ml/1-pt ice trays, cover with foil and freeze for 1 hour, until it is beginning to set. Transfer to a chilled bowl and beat well to break down the ice crystals. Fold in the egg whites, return to the ice trays, cover and freeze for a further 2 hours, or until firm.
    Leave the sorbet at room temperature for 10-15 minutes before spooning into chilled glasses. Pour a little kirsch, if using, over each one and decorate with geranium leaves.
    Make a raspberry sorbet in the same way, using fresh or frozen fruit in place of the blueberries. Garnish the sorbet with whipped cream and wafer biscuits, as in the photograph on page 114. Pour a little kirsch over if you wish.

CALIFORNIAN FRUIT SALAD

Photograph on page 102

No matter what the time of year, there is always a rich selection of fruits for a zingy salad to serve with cream, ice cream, or other rich desserts.

225 g/8 oz green grapes,
    seeded
225 g/8 oz black grapes,
    seeded
2 oranges, segmented
2 dessert apples, cored and
    thinly sliced
2 bananas, sliced
50 g/2 oz Brazil nuts, halved
Syrup
150 ml/¼ pt light red wine
45 ml/3 tbls clear honey
15 ml/1 tbls lemon juice
2 large bay leaves

Serves 6

Make a syrup by boiling the wine, honey, lemon juice and bay leaves with 150 ml/¼ pt water for 5 minutes, stirring to dissolve the honey. Discard the bay leaves.
    Mix together all the fruit, pour over the syrup and toss well. Stir in the nuts just before serving.

MANGO AND HONEY MOUSSE

Photograph on page 102

An exotic-tasting dessert, with a hint of the Caribbean, that is quick and easy to make.

2 large ripe mangoes
15 g/½ oz powdered gelatine
30 ml/2 tbls lemon juice
30 ml/2 tbls orange juice
30 ml/2 tbls clear honey
150 ml/¼ pt double cream,
    whipped
2 egg whites, stiffly whisked
fruit slices, to decorate (see
    method)

Serves 4

Halve the mangoes, remove the seeds and cut the flesh from the skin. Liquidize in a blender, then rub through a sieve. Dissolve the gelatine in the lemon and orange juice and stir into the fruit purée with the honey. Fold in the cream, then the egg whites.

Divide the mousse between 4 individual serving dishes and chill in the refrigerator. Decorate with slices of fresh mango, lemon or orange.

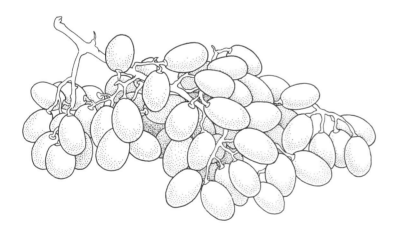

BANANA AND HONEY ICE CREAM CONES

Photograph on page 102

This is a fabulous dessert for children.

500 g/1 lb bananas
150 ml/¼ pt double cream
150 m/¼ pt plain yoghurt
30 ml/2 tbls lemon juice
75 ml/5 tbls set honey
125 g/4 oz crushed praline
    (facing page)
2 egg whites, stiffly beaten
50 g/2 oz pecan halves
12 ice-cream cones

Makes 12 cones

Mash the bananas and beat in the cream, yoghurt, lemon juice, honey and crushed praline. Turn into an ice cube tray, cover and freeze for 1 hour, until partly set. Transfer to a chilled bowl and beat well to break down the ice crystals. Fold in the egg whites, return to the container, cover and freeze for a further 2-3 hours, until firm.

Leave the ice cream in the refrigerator for 30 minutes before serving. Scoop it into the cones and arrange them on a serving dish.

ORANGE SORBET

Photograph on page 114

Citrus fruit sorbets look very pretty served in hollowed-out orange, lemon or grapefruit shells. You can freeze these for use again and again.

175 g/6 oz caster sugar
grated rind and juice of 4
    oranges
2 egg whites, stiffly beaten
slices of orange and fan-
    shaped wafer biscuits, to
    garnish
60 ml/4 tbls Calvados
    (optional), to serve

Serves 4

Put the sugar into a small pan with 600 ml/1 pt water, stir over low heat until the sugar has dissolved, then increase the heat. Boil for 10 minutes, remove from the heat and stir in the orange rind and juice. Set aside to cool (transfer to a bowl and stand it in iced water to hasten the process).

Pour the chilled mixture into an ice cube tray, cover and freeze for 1 hour, until it is mushy. Transfer to a chilled bowl, beat well to break down the ice crystals and fold in the egg whites. Return to the container, cover and freeze for a further 2 hours, or until firm.

Leave at room temperature for a few minutes before serving. Scoop into chilled individual dishes or citrus fruit shells, pour over the Calvados, and decorate with orange slices or mint sprigs.

To make lemon sorbet, use the rind and juice of 2 lemons in place of the oranges. Garnish with very thin strips of lemon peel which have been simmered for 15 minutes, drained and dried, and with a wafer biscuit.

UPSIDE-DOWN APPLE CHEESECAKE

The crumble topping makes a crisp golden crust over the filling of sliced apples; pears would be equally tasty.

250 g/8 oz full-fat cream
   cheese
150 ml/¼ pt plain yoghurt, or
   soured cream
25 g/1 oz cornflour
   (cornstarch)
50 g/2 oz caster sugar
grated rind and juice of 1
   lemon
grated rind and juice of 1
   orange
2 eggs, separated
75 g/3 oz seedless raisins
Topping
50 g/2 oz flour
5 ml/1 tsp ground ginger
1.5 ml/¼ tsp ground allspice
40 g/1½ oz butter
40 g/1½ oz soft light brown
   sugar
3 dessert apples

Serves 8

Beat together the cheese, yoghurt or soured cream, cornflour, caster sugar, lemon and orange rind and juice, and egg yolks until the mixture is smooth, then stir in the raisins. Whisk the egg whites until stiff and fold into the cheese mixture. Pour into a greased loose-bottomed 20-cm/8-in cake tin and level the top. Bake in the oven at 180C/350F/gas 4 for 45 minutes.

Sift together the flour, ginger and allspice and rub in the butter. Stir in the sugar. Core and slice 2 apples and arrange them over the cheesecake. Sprinkle on the crumb topping. Bake in the oven for a further 20 minutes until the topping is crisp. Leave to cool. Core and slice the remaining apple and arrange on top. Brush the slices with lemon juice to preserve their color. Serve chilled.

NEW YORK BAKED CHEESECAKE

There must be as many recipes aspiring to this description as there are people who cook them, so be adventurous with your own variations.

75 g/3 oz butter
50 g/2 oz caster sugar
175 g/6 oz digestive biscuits
   (graham crackers), finely
   crushed
Filling
250 g/8 oz full-fat cream
   cheese
3 large eggs, separated
5 ml/1 tsp vanilla essence
125 g/4 oz caster sugar
25 g/1 oz flour
150 ml/¼ pt double cream,
   stiffly whipped
300 ml/½ pt soured cream
75 g/3 oz mixed candied peel,
   chopped

Serves 8

Melt the butter and sugar over low heat, stirring until the sugar has dissolved. Remove from the heat and stir in the biscuit crumbs. Press the mixture into a greased 20-cm/8-in cake tin and chill in the refrigerator.

Beat the cheese and beat in the egg yolks one at a time, then the vanilla essence, half the sugar, and the flour. Beat well, then fold in the whipped cream and half of the soured cream. Stir in the peel.

Pour the filling into the tin and bake in the oven at 160C/325F/gas 3 for 1½ hours, or until the filling is set.

Cool in the tin. Turn out the cheesecake, beat the remaining soured cream and spread evenly over the top. Serve chilled.

PEACH CHEESECAKE

Topped with pecan halves and oozing with maple syrup, this cheesecake couldn't be anything but American!

50 g/2 oz butter
30 ml/2 tbls maple syrup
25 g/1 oz caster sugar
150 g/5 oz ginger snap
  biscuits, finely crushed
Filling
2 × 425-g/15-oz cans peach
  slices, drained
60 ml/4 tbls maple syrup
250 g/8 oz full-fat cream
  cheese
2 large eggs, separated
125 g/4 oz caster sugar
grated rind and juice of ½
  orange
150 ml/¼ pt soured cream
30 ml/2 tbls powdered
  gelatine
50 g/2 oz pecan halves

Serves 8

Melt the butter, syrup and sugar over low heat, stirring until the sugar has dissolved. Remove from the heat. Tip in the biscuit crumbs and stir well. Press the mixture into the base of a greased 20-cm/8-in cake tin and chill in the refrigerator.

Liquidize the drained peach slices from one can together with the maple syrup. Beat the cheese and beat in the egg yolks one at a time, then half the sugar, and the orange rind, peach purée and soured cream. Put the orange juice into a small bowl, sprinkle on the gelatine and stand it in a pan of hot water for 5 minutes, stirring occasionally to dissolve. Pour the gelatine into the cheese mixture and beat it well. Leave in a cool place for about 20 minutes until the filling starts to thicken.

Whisk the egg whites until stiff and fold in the remaining sugar. Fold into the cheese mixture. Pour the filling into the tin, level the top and chill for 4 hours, until the filling has set. Turn out the cheesecake.

Arrange the peach slices in a wheel pattern on top, with the pecan halves between them. Serve chilled.

STRAWBERRY JELLO CHEESECAKE

A convenience-food recipe, using a packet of fruit jelly to set and flavor the mixture. Delicious, though.

50 g/2 oz butter
25 g/1 oz caster sugar
125 g/4 oz chocolate-coated
  digestive biscuits (graham
  crackers), crushed
Filling
1 packet strawberry jelly
  (jello)
250 g/8 oz full-fat soft cheese
2 eggs, separated
125 g/4 oz caster sugar
300 ml/½ pt double cream,
  whipped
250 g/8 oz fresh strawberries

Serves 8

Melt the butter and sugar, stirring until the sugar has dissolved. Tip in the crumbs, mix well and press into a 20-cm/8-in greased cake tin. Chill in the refrigerator.

Break the jelly into squares and stir in 150 ml/¼ pt boiling water, until the jelly has dissolved. Set aside to cool. Beat the cheese and beat in the egg yolks one at a time. Beat in half of the sugar and slowly pour on the cooled jelly, stirring all the time. Fold in half of the cream. Set aside in a cool place for about 20 minutes, until the mixture is beginning to set.

Beat the egg whites until stiff and fold in the remaining sugar. Fold into the jelly mixture and pour onto the biscuit base. Level the top. Chill in the refrigerator for about 2 hours to set. Turn out onto a serving plate.

Pipe the remaining cream around the base and top of the cheesecake and decorate with strawberries. Serve chilled.

PEAR BEEHIVES

Photograph opposite

You don't have to be busy as a bee to make these pear pastries, but the family compliments will be buzzing!

4 firm pears
30 ml/2 tbls ground hazelnuts
3 gingersnap biscuits,
  crushed
100 g/4 oz clear honey
225 g/8 oz shortcrust pastry
  (page 105)
milk, for brushing
grated rind and juice of 1
  lemon

Serves 4

With a sharp, pointed knife, remove the core from the base of each pear. Mix together the ground hazelnuts and ginger crumbs with 15 ml/1 tbls of the honey and fill the cavities in the pears.

Roll out the pastry on a lightly-floured board and cut into strips 1 cm/½-in wide. Dampen the strips along one edge.

Starting at the base of each pear, twist the pastry in an overlapping coil to enclose the fruit completely, leaving only the stalks free. Press the pastry tightly around the pears.

Place on a baking sheet and brush with milk. Bake in the oven at 190C/375F/gas 5 for 20 minutes, or until the pastry is golden.

Warm the remaining honey with the lemon rind and juice and spoon over the pears. Serve hot with whipped cream.

PANCAKES

Pancakes, those popular descendants of the early griddle cakes, get better all the time! Serve them as Crêpes Suzette (below); filled with blueberries and cream; with cream cheese and flaked toasted almonds; with maple syrup or topped with ice cream. Whichever way, they're winners!

100 g/4 oz flour
a pinch of salt
2 eggs
300 ml/½ pt milk
white vegetable fat, for frying

Serves 4

Sift the flour and salt, beat in the eggs one at a time, then a little of the milk. Beat until smooth, then stir in the remainder of the milk and beat until bubbly. Or whizz the whole lot in a blender or food processor.

Melt a very small knob of fat in an omelette pan and tip it to cover the base. When a slight haze rises, pour in 30-45 ml/2-3 tbls of the batter, tilting the pan so that it spreads evenly. Cook over moderate-high heat for 1 minute, until the underside is brown.

Toss or flip over and cook until the other side is equally brown. Keep each pancake warm while you cook the remainder.
* For sweet pancakes, you can add 15 ml/1 tbls caster sugar to the batter, beating it in with the remaining milk. A little grated orange or lemon rind makes a tasty addition, too.
* For non-dairy meals (in Jewish cookery for example) substitute unsweetened orange juice for the milk.

APPLE FRITTERS

A real homestead family dessert which can be made extra special with a dash of spirit.

500 g/1 lb cooking apples,
    peeled, cored and sliced
    into 12-mm/½-in thick
    rings
butter, for shallow frying
caster sugar to serve
60 ml/4 tbls Calvados or
    lemon juice, to serve
Batter
125 g/4 oz flour
a pinch of salt
2 egg yolks
15 ml/1 tbls vegetable oil
150 ml/¼ pt milk
1 egg white, stiffly beaten

Serves 4

To make the batter, sift the flour and salt, make a well in the center, add the egg yolks and melted butter and gradually pour on the milk, beating all the time. Beat until smooth. Just before cooking, fold in the egg white.

Dip the apple rings in the batter. Heat the butter in a frying-pan and fry the apple rings in a single layer until golden brown on one side. Flip them over and fry the second side. Drain them on kitchen paper and keep them warm while you fry the remainder.

Serve very hot with a dusting of caster sugar, and with Calvados or lemon juice.

CRÊPES SUZETTE

It looks so simple when adroit waiters toss and turn them in the restaurant. And you'll be delighted to discover that it is!

8 pancakes
75 g/3 oz butter
75 g/3 oz caster sugar
grated rind of 1 lemon
grated rind and juice of ½
    orange
60 ml/4 tbls Cointreau
30 ml/2 tbls brandy

Serves 4

Melt the butter in a frying-pan and stir in the sugar. When it has dissolved, add the lemon and orange rind and the orange juice and bring to the boil. Add the liqueur and boil until the mixture is syrupy.

Fold each pancake into 4, making a wedge shape and add them to the sauce. Spoon it over the pancakes and heat them through.

Heat the brandy, pour it over the pancakes and light it. Serve at once.

PLUM CUSTARDS

As each fruit season comes around, here is a super family way to serve it – perched on top of creamy custard.

500 g/1 lb red plums, stoned.
50 g/2 oz sugar
450 ml/¾ pt milk
1 vanilla pod
3 eggs
150 ml/¼ pt double cream,
   whipped
30 ml/2 tbls split blanched
   almonds, toasted

Serves 4

Put the plums in a shallow pan with 30 ml/2 tbls water and all but 30 ml/2 tbls sugar. Cover and simmer very gently, shaking the pan occasionally, until the fruit is tender. Arrange half the plums in a 1-liter/1¾-pt ovenproof dish.

Heat the milk with the vanilla pod. Lightly beat the eggs with the remaining sugar and strain on the milk, beating all the time. Pour over the fruit and cover with foil.

Stand the dish in a roasting tin with 5 cm/2-in cold water. Cook in the oven at 170C/325F/gas 3 for 1 hour, or until the custard is firm. Cool, then chill in the refrigerator.

Pipe whipped cream to decorate the top and arrange the toasted almonds. Spoon the plums into the center. Serve chilled.

PEARS IN CRANBERRY SAUCE

Cranberry sauce gives a tempting glow to poached pears. This is an "either/or" dessert – you can serve it hot or cold.

8 small ripe pears
250 g/8 oz whole-berry
   cranberry sauce
90 ml/6 tbls red wine
1.5 ml/¼ tsp ground
   cinnamon
grated rind and juice of 1
   orange
60 ml/4 tbls blanched
   almonds, toasted

Serves 4

Peel the pears, without removing the stalks. Mix together the cranberry sauce, wine, cinnamon, orange rind and juice, pour into a shallow pan and add the pears. Baste them with the sauce and simmer very gently for 15 minutes, basting occasionally, or until the pears are tender.

Arrange the pears in a serving dish, pour the sauce over and scatter on the almonds. Serve with soured cream or whipped double cream.

RASPBERRY AND ORANGE MERINGUE

Photograph opposite

The perfect dessert to take to a "bring a dish" party. The only trouble is it's taking unfair advantage of the other cooks!

5 ml/1 tsp cornflour
  (cornstarch)
5 ml/1 tsp vanilla essence
5 ml/1 tsp white distilled
  vinegar
3 egg whites
225 g/7 oz caster sugar
50 g/2 oz unsalted butter,
  softened
100 g/4 oz icing sugar, sifted
grated rind of 1 orange
5 ml/1 tsp orange juice
250 g/8 oz fresh raspberries,
  hulled
150 ml/¼ pt double cream,
  whipped

Serves 6-8

Blend the cornflour, vanilla and vinegar until smooth. Whisk the egg whites until they are very stiff and dry. Whisk in 50 g/2 oz of the caster sugar, then fold in the remainder, with the cornflour mixture.

Cover a baking sheet with non-stick baking parchment. Spread the meringue mixture to make a 22.5-cm/9-in circle. Bake in the oven at 140C/275F/gas 1 for 1 hour. Switch off heat and leave meringue to cool in the oven for 1 hour. Cool completely on a wire rack, then peel off the paper.

For the topping, beat together the butter and icing sugar, add the orange rind and beat in the juice drop by drop. Fold in the cream.

Spread the topping over the meringue and top with raspberries. Serve with whipped cream.

7: BAKING

If we melt butter on to piping hot golden corn bread, split a piece of pitta and fill it with barbecued meat, wrap a pancake round a savory filling or drop spoonfuls of batter to bubble and set into tasty drop scones on a hot pan, we are enjoying the various forms of unleavened bread that early Americans cooked of necessity. Even that must have been uphill work for the Colonists, who had been in the habit of buying their bread and cakes from licensed bakers back home.

Corn, the indigenous crop of America, was unfamiliar to the English settlers, who had to grind it to a coarse meal between two stones, and, often even without salt (which was in short supply) turn it into the staff of a grueling life. Flat cakes of dough were baked on a hot iron over the fire or actually in the ashes. These early corn breads have romantic, evocative names – ashcake, Johnny (or journey) cake, hoe cake and corn pone among them.

As crops of rye, oats and wheat were produced, the horizons of baking expanded, though lightness of texture was still an elusive quality. Housewives and cowboy bakers alike had to create their own raising agent, since baking powder was not introduced until 1856 and commercial yeast even later, in 1868. There were two ways of doing this. One was to blend corn meal, sugar and water, leave the mixture to ferment overnight, then stir it with flour, salt and any flavorings to produce a "salt-rising" bread.

The other method, for sour-dough bread, involved making a wild yeast starter from a variety of ingredients and keeping the mixture topped up each time a little was used. The sour-dough technique requires a nicety of timing and an eye on the temperature, and tales abound of diligent wagon cooks wrapping their pot of starter in blankets at night to protect the following day's bread supply.

With the availability of commercial raising agents and milled white flours - robbed of the bran and germ - baking literally rose to new heights, progressing through soda breads, baking powder biscuits (which the British call scones) and muffins, to light-as-a-feather confections such as angel cake and chiffon pie.

For better or worse, commerce took home baking in hand and nowhere in the world can one buy a larger or more delicious range of packaged cake mixes than in the United States. With tempting packets promising guaranteed success with maple walnut, butterscotch, chocolate mint, coffee marble, strawberry and countless other flavors, home cooking has never been easier.

In this chapter we turn the spotlight on America's early baking successes - corn bread, steamed Boston brown bread, pumpkin bread and bran muffins – cookies and crunchy bars for the cookie jar, and tray bakes which are so easy and delicious to take to a bring-a-dish party, a charity event or on a picnic.

128

LEMON FANS

Crunchy golden granulated sugar and tangy lemon rind make these very acceptable "gift bakes".

125 g/4 oz butter
75 g/3 oz golden granulated
  sugar
150 g/6 oz flour
45 ml/3 tbls cornflour
2.5 ml/½ tsp salt
2.5 ml/½ tsp baking powder
grated rind of ½ lemon

Makes 8 slices

Cream together the butter and 65 g/2½ oz of the sugar until the mixture is soft. Sift together the flour, cornflour, salt and baking powder and gradually beat the dry ingredients into the butter mixture.

Press the mixture into a greased and floured 180-mm/7-in flan ring on a baking tray and level the top. Prick all over with a fork. Mix the lemon rind with the remaining sugar and sprinkle over the dough.

Bake in the oven at 160C/325F/gas 3 for 45 minutes. Score into 8 segments and cool in the tin. Store in an airtight container.

SPICED APPLE SQUARES

Photograph opposite

175 g/6 oz margarine
175 g/6 oz light Muscovado
  sugar
3 eggs
15 ml/1 tbls honey
250 g/8 oz self-raising flour
10 ml/2 tsp ground ginger
2.5 ml/½ tsp ground
  cinnamon
500 g/1 lb cooking apples,
  peeled, cored and finely
  chopped
Topping (optional)
150 ml/¼ pt soured cream
5 ml/1 tsp grated lemon rind

Makes one 20-cm/8-in tin

Cream together the margarine and sugar until light. Beat in the eggs one at a time, then the honey. Sift together the flour and spices and gradually add them to the sugar mixture, beating all the time. Stir in the chopped apples.

Turn the mixture into a greased and lined baking tin 20 cm/8 in square and level the top. Bake in the oven at 180C/350F/gas 4 for 1½ hours. Cut into squares and leave to cool in the tin.

For the topping, whip the soured cream, stir in the lemon rind and spread over the squares.

SULTANA SQUARES

Photograph opposite

It's easy to take a tin of spicy bakes on a picnic or a visit.

375 g/12 oz self-raising flour
salt
2.5 ml/½ tsp ground
  cinnamon
175 g/6 oz margarine
175 g/6 oz light Muscovado
  sugar
1.5 ml/¼ tsp grated nutmeg
75 g/3 oz sultanas
2 eggs
60 ml/4 tbls milk

Makes one 15-cm/6-in tin

Sift together the flour, salt and cinnamon and rub in the margarine until the mixture is like fine breadcrumbs. Stir in the sugar, nutmeg and sultanas. Beat in the eggs and enough of the milk to form a stiff dough.

Turn the mixture into a greased and lined 15-cm/6-in square baking tin. Bake in the oven at 180C/350F/gas 4 for 1½ hours. Cut into squares and cool in the tin.

CHOCOLATE CAKE WITH FANTASTIC FROSTING

A moist cake with an American "fantastic frosting". It's ideal for a gala family tea.

250 g/8 oz butter, softened
275 g/9 oz molasses sugar
125 ml/4 fl oz corn oil
4 eggs
200 g/6 oz self-raising flour
50 g/2 oz cocoa
Frosting
200 g/6 oz sugar
5 ml/1 tsp cornflour
6 egg yolks, lightly beaten
250 g/8 oz butter, softened
salt
2.5 ml/½ tsp vanilla essence
125 g/4 oz almond paste,
  finely chopped
50 g/2 oz bitter chocolate,
  melted
45 ml/3 tbls blanched
  almonds, toasted

Serves 10

Cream together the butter, sugar and oil until well blended. Beat in the eggs one at a time, alternately with a little of the flour. Sift the remaining flour and cocoa and fold into the butter mixture. Divide between two 20-cm/8-in greased and lined sandwich tins.

Bake in the oven at 180C/350F/gas 4 for 30 minutes. Cool slightly in the tins, then turn out onto a wire rack.

To make the frosting, put the sugar, cornflour and 175 ml/6 fl oz water into a pan and bring to the boil. Boil until the syrup reaches 114C/238F. Pour the syrup slowly onto the egg yolks, beating constantly until light and fluffy. Beat in the butter a little at a time and stir in the salt and vanilla.

Take out one third of the mixture and beat the chopped almond paste into it. Sandwich the two cake layers together with this filling.

Beat the melted chocolate into the remaining frosting. Spread over the top and sides of the cake. Decorate with toasted almonds. Store in the refrigerator for up to one day.

BANANA AND YOGHURT CAKE

125 g/4 oz margarine
300 g/10 oz golden granulated
  sugar
2 eggs, beaten
375 g/12 oz self-raising flour
5 ml/1 tsp bicarbonate of soda
2.5 ml/½ tsp salt
2 ripe bananas, mashed
45 ml/3 tbls plain yoghurt
5 ml/1 tsp vanilla essence
50 g/2 oz pecans, chopped
Filling
2 ripe bananas
5 ml/1 tsp lemon juice
75 g/3 oz full-fat soft cheese
45 ml/3 tbls soured cream
icing sugar, to decorate

Serves 6-8

Cream the margarine and sugar until light, gradually add the eggs and beat well. Sift together the flour, soda and salt and beat into the sugar mixture a little at a time. Beat in the bananas, yoghurt and vanilla, and stir in the pecans.

Divide the mixture between two greased and lined 20-cm/ 8-in sandwich tins. Bake in the oven at 180C/350F/gas 4 for 35 minutes, or until well risen and golden brown. Cool slightly in the tins, then turn out onto a wire rack. For the filling, mash the bananas with the lemon juice. Beat the cheese, then gradually beat in the banana, then the soured cream. Sandwich the two layers together with the banana filling. Sift icing sugar over the top to decorate.

MUESLI FINGERS

The current popularity of healthy ingredients makes present-day favorites very like those enjoyed by early settlers.

60 ml/4 tbls corn oil
60 ml/4 tbls clear honey
75 g/3 oz light Muscovado
  sugar
150 g/5 oz oat flakes
30 ml/2 tbls sesame seeds
45 ml/3 tbls sunflower seeds
25 g/1 oz desiccated coconut
50 g/2 oz dried apricots,
  chopped
50 g/2 oz blanched almonds,
  chopped

Makes 20 fingers

Heat oil, honey and sugar over low heat, stirring occasionally, until the sugar has dissolved. Stir in the remaining ingredients and mix to form a dough. Knead lightly until smooth.

Press the dough into a greased baking tin 18×28 cm/7×11 in. Bake in the oven at 180C/350F/gas 4 for 20-25 minutes, until golden brown. Mark into fingers, then cool slightly in tin. Turn out onto a wire rack to cool. Store in an airtight tin.

SAVORY GRIDDLE CAKES

Photograph on page 126

An updated version of the pancakes early Americans used to cook on an iron griddle over the hot embers.

125 g/4 oz self-raising flour
salt
1 egg, lightly beaten
20 ml/4 tsp chive mustard
60 ml/4 tbls milk
butter or oil, for greasing

Makes 10-12 scones

Sift together the flour and salt, beat in the egg, mustard and milk and beat well.

Lightly grease a heavy-based frying-pan or a griddle iron and heat it. When it is hot drop 15 ml/1 tablespoons of the mixture well apart and cook over moderately high heat until golden brown. Flip over and cook the other side. Serve at once, with cream cheese or cottage cheese.

CARROT CAKE

or Passion cake, whichever you prefer to call it. This is a delicious example of Jewish cookery.

50 g/2 oz pecans, chopped
50 g/2 oz walnuts, chopped
2 ripe bananas, mashed
175 g/6 oz light Muscovado
    sugar
5 ml/1 tsp vanilla essence
3 eggs
300 g/12 oz flour
5 ml/1 tsp bicarbonate of soda
10 ml/2 tsp baking powder
10 ml/2 tsp ground cinnamon
200 ml/7 fl oz corn oil
175 g/6 oz carrots, peeled and
    grated
Frosting
75 g/3 oz full-fat cream cheese
50 g/2 oz butter
2.5 ml/½ tsp vanilla essence
125 g/4 oz sifted icing sugar

Makes one 22.5-cm/9-in cake

Mix together the nuts, bananas, sugar and vanilla and beat in the eggs one at a time. Sift together the flour, salt, soda, baking powder and cinnamon and gradually stir into the banana mixture. Stir in the oil, beat well, then stir in the carrots.

Turn the mixture into a greased and lined 22.5cm/9-in cake tin. Bake in the oven at 180C/350Fgas 4 for 65 minutes, until the cake is golden brown and spongy to the touch. Leave to cool for 5 minutes in the tin. Then turn out onto a wire rack.

To make the frosting, beat together the cheese, butter and vanilla and stir in the icing sugar. Beat until smooth.

When the cake is completely cold, spread the frosting over the top and sides. If liked, decorate the top with slices of fresh or candied orange.

MUSTARD BISCUITS, ALIAS SCONES

Photograph on page 126

250 g/8 oz wholewheat flour
5 ml/1 tsp baking powder
salt and pepper
75 g/3 oz butter
125 g/4 oz mature hard
   cheese, grated
30 ml/2 tbls chive mustard
75-90 ml/5-6 tbls plain
   yoghurt

Makes 12 scones

Sift together the flour, baking powder and salt. Tip in the bran
from the sieve and add a few grindings of pepper. Rub in the
butter until the mixture is like fine crumbs. Stir in three-
quarters of the cheese, the mustard and enough yoghurt to
make a firm dough. Knead lightly and roll out on a lightly-
floured board to 18 mm/¾ in thick. Cut into rounds with a
6.5-cm/2 ½-in cutter. Place the rounds on a greased baking
sheet and sprinkle with the remaining cheese. Bake in the
oven at 220C/425F/gas 7 for 12-15 minutes, until well risen and
golden. Serve warm if possible, split and buttered.

BAKING POWDER BISCUITS

Made in a trice, these American biscuits – or scones – are as
popular now as they ever were.

300 g/10 oz flour
10 ml/2 tsp baking powder
2.5 ml/½ tsp salt
200 ml/7 fl oz single cream
1 egg
a few drops of vanilla essence

Makes about 20 biscuits

Sift together the flour, baking powder and salt. Beat the cream,
egg and vanilla and gradually mix into the dry ingredients.
Mix lightly to form a dough. On a lightly-floured board, roll
out the dough to a thickness of 12 mm/½ in and cut into
5-cm/2-in rounds. Place on a greased baking sheet. Bake in the
oven at 200C/400F/gas 6 for 15 minutes, or until the biscuits
are pale golden brown. Serve hot, with butter and jam or
honey.

CHEESE BISCUITS

Photograph on page 126

A taste of the farmhouse, with cheese and buttermilk biscuits,
known as dairy scones in Britain.

250 g/8 oz self-raising flour
salt
a pinch of cayenne pepper
40 g/1½ oz butter
75 g/3 oz cheese such as
   Caerphilly, grated
150 ml/¼ pt buttermilk
milk, for brushing

Makes 10 scones

Sift together the flour, salt and cayenne and rub in the butter
until the mixture is like fine breadcrumbs. Stir in the cheese
and gradually pour on the buttermilk, mixing to a firm dough.
Knead lightly and roll out on a lightly-floured board to a
thickness of 12 mm/½ in. Cut into rounds with a 6,5-cm/
2½-in cutter and place on a greased baking tray. Brush the
tops with milk.
   Bake in the oven at 220C/425F/gas 7 for 10 minutes, until
well risen and golden brown. Serve hot if possible, with butter
and cheese.

PEANUT COOKIES

Photograph opposite

150 g/5 oz smooth peanut
   butter
75 g/3 oz soft margarine
200 g/7 oz golden granulated
   sugar
1 egg, lightly beaten
2.5 ml/½ tsp vanilla essence
150 g/5 oz flour
2/5 ml/½ tsp salt
2.5 ml/½ tsp bicarbonate of
   soda
30 ml/2 tbls unsalted peanuts,
   crushed

Makes about 40 cookies

Cream together the peanut butter and margarine and beat in
the sugar. Beat in the egg a little at a time, then the vanilla
essence. Sift together the flour, salt and soda and gradually
beat into the butter mixture. Stir in the crushed peanuts.
   Roll the dough into 2.5-cm/1-in diameter balls and place
them well apart on an ungreased baking sheet. Flatten them
with a fork, pressing in the tines to make a ridged pattern.
   Bake in the oven at 190C/375F/gas 5 for 10 minutes. Leave on
the sheet until the cookies harden, then transfer to a wire tray
to cool. Store in an airtight tin.

LACE COOKIES

These are light, crunchy cookies, tasty to serve at a coffee party.

125 g/4 oz unsalted butter
125g/4 oz sugar
125 g/4 oz rolled oats
salt
a few drops of vanilla essence

Makes about 24 cookies

Cream the butter and sugar until light and fluffy and stir in the oats, salt and vanilla. Form into a stiff dough. Roll the dough into balls about the size of a walnut and place well apart on a greased baking tray. Flatten each one slightly.

Bake in the oven at 200C/400F/gas 6 for 5-6 minutes, until the edges are golden brown. Cool slightly on the tray, then transfer to a wire rack. Store in an airtight tin.

MOCHA COOKIES

The word "cookies," so integral a part of American culinary terminology, originated from the Dutch word *koekjes*, the "little cakes" which the immigrants brought with them.

150 g/5 oz butter, softened
75 g/3 oz light Muscovado
    sugar
125 g/4 oz caster sugar
a pinch of salt
1 egg
20 ml/4 tsp instant coffee
    powder
30 ml/2 tbls corn oil
125 g/4 oz flour
175 g/6 oz chocolate dots
50 g/2 oz blanched almonds,
    chopped

Makes about 16 cookies

Cream the butter and sugars, beat in the salt, egg, coffee powder and oil. Sift in the flour and stir in the chocolate dots and nuts. Cover and chill for 20 minutes.

Drop 30-ml/2-tbls-sized portions of the mixture well apart onto greased baking sheets. Bake in the oven at 190C/375F/gas 5 for 10 minutes. Transfer to a wire rack to cool.

PUMPKIN MUFFINS

When you're making pumpkin pie, save a little to make these family muffins, delicious served warm with Apple butter (page 158).

175 g/6 oz steamed pumpkin,
    mashed
1 egg
120 ml/4 fl oz plain yoghurt
40 g/1½ oz butter, melted and
    cooled
175 g/6 oz self-raising flour
125 g/4 oz caster sugar
5 ml/1 tsp ground cinnamon
1.5 ml/¼ tsp grated nutmeg
50 g/2 oz seedless raisins
25 g/1 oz mixed candied peel,
    chopped

Makes 12 muffins

Mix together the pumpkin, egg, yoghurt and butter and beat until smooth. Sift together the flour, sugar and spices and stir into the pumpkin mixture. Stir in the peel and raisins and beat well.

Spoon the batter into 12 greased deep patty tins. Bake in the oven at 200C/400F/gas 6 for 20-25 minutes, until the muffins are well risen and golden brown. Cool slightly in the tins, then turn onto a wire rack. Serve warm, if possible.

BRAN MUFFINS

Sweet muffins have long been a favorite American breakfast. Serve them warm, spread with jam or canned pie filling.

50 g/2 oz all-bran cereal
150 ml/¼ pt milk
50 g/2 oz butter, softened
50 g/2 oz light Muscovado
    sugar
1 egg, beaten
25 g/1 oz walnuts, chopped
75 g/3 oz raisins
125 g/4 oz flour
20 ml/2 tsp baking powder
salt

Makes 18 muffins

Soak the cereal in the milk for 10 minutes. Beat in the butter, sugar, egg, walnuts and raisins. Sift together the flour, baking powder and salt and gradually stir into the bran mixture. Beat until smooth.

Spoon into 18 greased bun tins. Bake in the oven at 200C/400F/gas 6 for 20-25 minutes, until the muffins are golden brown and spongy to the touch. Serve warm. You can make the mixture and leave it in the refrigerator overnight, ready to bake in the morning.

GREAT LAKES PASTRY ROLLS

A speciality of Michigan, in the Great Lakes region, these fruit-filled yeast pastries are served at breakfast, dusted with sugar and eaten straight from the oven.

175 g/6 oz butter
75 g/3 oz sugar
1 egg, lightly beaten
5 ml/1 tsp grated lemon rind
salt
75 ml/5 tbls milk, lukewarm
5 g/¼ oz dried yeast
250 g/8 oz flour
2 cooking apples, peeled,
  cored and finely chopped
125 g/5 oz dried stoned dates,
  finely chopped
75 g/3 oz Brazil nuts, finely
  chopped
icing sugar, for dusting

Makes about 20 pastries

Melt 125 g/4 oz of the butter and stir in the sugar. Leave the remaining butter to soften at room temperature. Beat the egg, lemon rind, salt and milk into the sugar mixture. Mix the yeast with 75 ml/5 tbls warm water, stir well and set aside for about 15 minutes, until it is frothy. Sift the flour into a bowl and beat in the sugar and yeast mixtures. Beat until smooth, cover the bowl and chill in the refrigerator for at least 2 hours. Divide the dough in half. On a lightly-floured board roll each piece to a rectangle about 6-mm/

STICKY PEAR GINGERBREAD

An example of an American "upside-down" cake decorated with a colorful pattern of fruit in a sticky topping.

125 g/4 oz margarine
175 g/6 oz black treacle
50 g/2 oz corn syrup or golden
  syrup
50 g/2 oz light Muscovado
  sugar
150 ml/¼ pt milk
2 eggs, beaten
250 g/8 oz flour
10 ml/2 tsp mixed ground
  spice
10 ml/2 tsp ground ginger
5 ml/1 tsp bicarbonate of soda
Topping
2 dessert pears, peeled, cored
  and thinly sliced
50 g/2 oz unsalted butter
45 ml/3 tbls demerara sugar
a few drops of vanilla essence
30 ml/2 tbls glace cherries
candied angelica, to decorate

Serves 8

Grease a 20-cm/8-in cake tin. Arrange the pear slices to cover the base. Cream together the butter and demerara sugar and add the vanilla. Spread the mixture over the pears.

Heat the margarine, treacle, syrup and sugar over low heat, stirring occasionally, until it has melted. Remove from the heat, add the milk and cool slightly. Stir in the eggs.

Sift together the flour, spices and soda and gradually pour on the egg mixture. beating all the time. Slowly pour the mixture over the pears.

Bake in the oven at 150C/350F/gas 2 for 1¼ hours, or until the gingerbread is cooked. To test, insert a fine skewer – it should come out clean. Cool slightly in the tin. Turn the gingerbread onto a serving dish and decorate with the cherries and "leaves" cut from the angelica. Serve hot or cold.

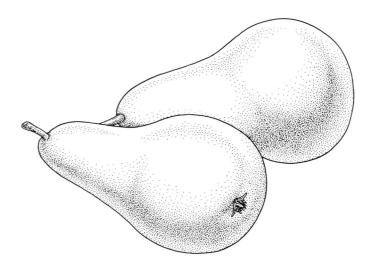

BUTTERMILK BISCUITS

Photograph opposite

From the American South, a recipe for "biscuits" which British cooks will recognize as scones.

250 g/8 oz flour
5 ml/1 tsp baking powder
1.5 ml/¼ tsp bicarbonate of
   soda
2.5 ml/½ tsp salt
50 g/2 oz butter
250 ml/9 fl oz buttermilk

Makes about 12 biscuits

Sift together the flour, baking powder, soda and salt. Rub in the butter until the mixture is like fine crumbs and pour on enough milk to make a soft but not sticky dough.
   Roll out on a lightly-floured board to 12 mm/½ in thick and cut into rounds with a 6.5-cm/2½-in cutter. Place on a greased baking sheet. Bake in the oven at 220C/425F/gas 7 for 12-15 minutes, until well risen and golden brown. Serve, warm if possible, with whipped cream and soft fruits.

DOUGHNUTS

Many Americans now experience the delights of sugary-coated doughnuts only from the cook-in store. Here's how to make them.

250 g/8 oz flour
a pinch of salt
2.5 ml/½ tsp baking powder
2.5 ml/½ tsp ground
    cinnamon
50 g/2 oz butter, melted
2 eggs, beaten
75 ml/5 tbls sugar
150 ml/¼ pt milk, lukewarm
oil, for deep frying
Coating
60 ml/4 tbls caster sugar
125 g/4 oz icing sugar, sifted
10 ml/2 tsp orange juice
5 ml/1 tsp grated orange rind
40 g/1½ oz walnuts, chopped

Makes 12 doughnuts

Sift together the flour, salt, baking powder and cinnamon. Mix together the melted butter, eggs and sugar and slowly pour on to the flour, stirring constantly. Pour on the milk, still stirring, and mix to form a stiff dough. Divide the dough into 12 pieces, shape each one into a sausage 10 cm/4 in long, brush the ends with milk and pinch them together to form a circle.

   Heat oil for deep frying to 180C/350F and cook the doughnuts a few at a time until they are well risen and golden brown. Lift them from the oil with a draining spoon and dip them in caster sugar to coat one side. Leave them to cool and cook the remaining dough in the same way.

   Mix the icing sugar with the orange juice and orange rind and a very little water, to make glacé icing. When the doughnuts are cold, spread the icing on the unsugared sides and sprinkle with the nuts.

PUMPKIN BREAD

A traditional American bread served on the last Thursday in November.

500 g/1 lb pumpkin, peeled
    and diced
500 g/1 lb soft dark brown
    sugar
150 ml/¼ pt vegetable oil
2.5 ml/½ tsp vanilla essence
300 g/10 oz wholewheat flour
5 ml/1 tsp ground cinnamon
2.5 ml/½ tsp ground cloves
2.5 ml/½ tsp salt
7.5 ml/1½ tsp bicarbonate of
    soda
125 g/4 oz stoned dates,
    chopped

Makes two 500-g/1-lb loaves

Steam the pumpkin over boiling water for 20-25 minutes, or until it is tender. Mash it thoroughly and allow to cool. Beat together the pumpkin, sugar, oil and vanilla essence until smooth. Sift the flour, spices, salt and soda and tip in the bran remaining in the sieve. Stir in the dates. Gradually stir the dry ingredients into the pumpkin mixture. Beat until smooth.

   Turn the mixture into two greased 500-g/1-lb loaf tins. Bake at 180C/350F/gas 4 for 1 hour, or until a skewer pierced through the center of a loaf comes out clean. Cover with foil if the loaves brown too quickly. Stand the tins on a wire rack to cool. Turn out and serve cold. The bread is delicious sliced and spread with butter beaten with grated orange rind and a pinch of ground cinnamon.

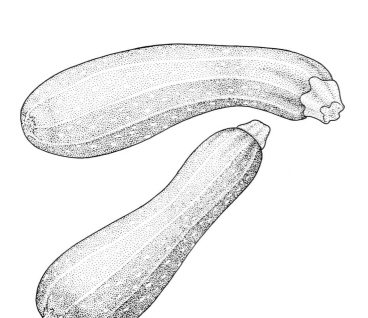

COURGETTE AND WALNUT TEABREAD

Photograph on page 126

Sliced and spread with butter or cream cheese, this moist loaf is good with soup and salad.

175 g/6 oz flour
10 ml/2 tsp baking powder
5 ml/1 tsp salt
10 ml/2 tsp caster sugar
175 g/6 oz courgettes, grated
75 g/3 oz walnuts, chopped
2 eggs
60 ml/4 tbls vegetable oil
45 ml/3 tbls chive mustard

Makes 12 slices

Sift the flour, baking powder, salt and sugar and stir in the courgettes and walnuts. Beat together the eggs, oil and mustard and stir them into the dry ingredients. Beat well.

   Turn the mixture into a greased and lined 0.75-liter/1½-pt loaf tin. Bake in the oven at 180C/350F/gas 4 for 1 hour, until the loaf is well risen and firm to the touch. Cool slightly in the tin, then transfer to a wire rack. Serve cold.

SODA BREAD

In the hectic early days of establishing a new community, there wasn't always time to wait for yeast dough to rise - nor, sometimes, is there nowadays.

1 kg/2¼ lb strong white bread
   flour
500 g/1 lb wholewheat flour
20 ml/4 tsp salt
20 ml/4 tsp bicarbonate of
   soda
15 ml/1 tbls caster sugar
125 g/4 oz butter
600 ml/1 pt buttermilk
4 eggs, beaten
milk, for brushing
30 ml/2 tbls cracked wheat

Makes two 750-g/1½-lb
   loaves

Sift together the flours, salt, soda and sugar and tip in the bran remaining in the sieve. Rub in the butter until it is evenly distributed. Mix together the buttermilk and eggs and gradually pour on to the dry ingredients, stirring constantly. Shape into a firm dough and knead lightly.

Divide the dough in half, shape each piece into a round and place on a greased baking sheet. Flatten slightly and mark a cross on top, using the back of a knife blade. Brush with milk and sprinkle with cracked wheat.

Bake in the oven at 220C/425F/gas 7 for 25 minutes. The loaves should sound hollow when tapped. Serve the same day.

CORN BREAD

A traditional bread, also known as Johnny cake (or journey cake), that was baked on a griddle over an open fire. Serve it to accompany breakfast or main-meal dishes, or spread with butter and maple syrup at tea-time.

175 g/6 oz corn meal, or
   polenta
250 g/8 oz flour
15 ml/1 tbls baking powder
5 ml/1 tsp salt
75 g/3 oz sugar
225 ml/8 fl oz plain yoghurt
60 ml/4 tbls buttermilk
1 egg, well beaten
25 g/1 oz butter, melted and
   cooled

Makes one 20 × 20-cm/8 ×
   8-in loaf

Sift together the corn meal, flour, baking powder, salt and sugar. Mix the yoghurt, buttermilk, egg and melted butter and gradually pour on to the dry ingredients, beating constantly. Pour the mixture into a greased 20 × 30-cm/8×8-in baking tin. Bake in the oven at 220C/425F/gas 7 for 20 minutes. Serve warm if possible.

BOSTON BROWN BREAD

The chapter heading "baking" allows a little licence - this New England rye bread is actually steamed. It's traditionally served with Boston baked beans.

125 g/4 oz rye flour
125 g/4 oz corn meal
125 g/4 oz wholewheat flour
2.5 ml/½ tsp baking powder
2.5 ml/½ tsp bicarbonate of
   soda
5 ml/1 tsp salt
300 ml/½ pt buttermilk
100 ml/3½ fl oz molasses

Serves 8

Sift the flours with the baking powder, soda and salt and tip in any bran remaining in the sieve. Mix together the buttermilk and molasses and gradually stir into the dry ingredients.

Pour the batter into a well-greased 1-liter/2-pt pudding bowl. Cover with a piece of greased foil pleated across the center to allow for expansion. Place on a rack in a covered pan of boiling water, cover and steam for 2½ hours, topping up with more boiling water as needed. Leave the bread to cool a little in the bowl, then turn on to a wire rack. Serve cold, sliced and buttered.

BREAKFAST LOAF

Cereal and dried fruit baked into a quick and easy loaf can make a pleasant change for breakfast. Spread with cottage cheese, cream cheese or butter.

125 g/4 oz all-bran cereal
125 g/4 oz light Muscovado
   sugar
125 g/4 oz sultanas
125 g/4 oz seedless raisins
75 g/3 oz dried apricots,
   chopped
300 ml/½ pt milk
125 g/4 oz self-raising flour

Makes one 1-kg/2-lb loaf

Put the cereal, sugar, dried fruits and milk into a bowl, mix well and set aside for 30 minutes. Sift in the flour and beat well. Turn the mixture into a greased 1-kg/2-lb loaf tin. Bake in the oven at 180C/350F/gas 4 for 1 hour. Cool slightly in the tin, then turn out onto a wire rack.

A BATCH OF BREAD

Photograph opposite

Good wholesome bread is a staple part of America's heritage.
Here's a fast-rising method that snips minutes off the waiting
time.

1.5 kg/3¼ lb wholewheat
   plain flour
25 g/1 oz dried yeast
50 mg tablet Vitamin C,
   crushed
15 ml/1 tbls light Muscovado
   sugar
900 ml/1½ pt warm water
25 g/1 oz butter, grated
15 ml/1 tbls salt
Glaze
1 egg, beaten
5 ml/1 tsp sugar

Makes one 750-g/1½-lb loaf, 8
   rolls and 8 crescents

Put the yeast, Vitamin C tablet and 5 ml/1 tsp of the sugar into
a bowl, stir in 300 ml/½ pt of the water and whisk well.
Set aside in a warm place for 10-15 minutes until the mixture is
frothy.

Take out 60 ml/4 tbls of the flour. Tip the remainder into a
bowl with the rest of the sugar, the butter and salt and stir in
the water. Add the yeast mixture and stir well. Shape into a
dough.

Sprinkle flour on a board and onto your hands and knead
until the dough is smooth and elastic, sprinkling on more flour
if needed. Divide the dough into three.

Shape one piece to fit a greased and lined baking tin - the
photograph shows an earthenware crock. Divide another
piece of dough into 8 and shape into rounds for rolls. Place on
a greased baking sheet. Roll the remaining piece of dough to a
rectangle about 65×40 cm /25×15 in. Cut it into 3 strips, each
one about 65×13 cm/25×5 in and cut each strip into 5
triangles.

Roll up each one loosely from the base to the point, with the
tip underneath. Curve into crescent shapes and place on a
greased baking sheet.

Mix the egg and sugar glaze with 15 ml/1 tbls water and
brush over the loaf and rolls. Cover the dough with polythene
and leave in a warm place for 30 minutes to rise. Remove the
covering.

Pre-heat the oven to 230C/450F/gas 8. Bake the loaf for 35
minutes, until the underside sounds hollow when tapped.

Sprinkle cracked wheat over the rolls. Reduce the heat to
190C/375F/gas 5 and bake them in the oven for 25-30 minutes.
Transfer them to a baking tray to cool.

Bake the crescent rolls in the oven at the same temperature
for 25-30 minutes and cool them on a baking sheet.

8: SNACKS

The very mention of the words "snacks" and "snacking" conjures up images of 20th-century impatiences, unhealthy foods snatched up and devoured by people without a moment to spare. Not necessarily so! Snacks may be prepared in a trice on modern appliances, even eaten standing up – both at a cocktail party and on the touch-line - but they can perfectly well be made with *real* ingredients. And they have a respectable and ancient lineage.

Take popcorn, that puff of golden cereal that is synonymous with today's hasty way of life. A leading botanist has traced its genealogy and assures us that, "the original corn – wild corn and early cultivated corn – was popcorn, and it is quite probable that the first use man made of corn was by "popping." Tempting though it was, not all of this inflatable corn was eaten. Columbus found the natives in the West Indies selling popcorn decorations like baseball or football favors, and the Aztec Indians used it as necklaces and to decorate ceremonial headdresses and the statues of their gods.

Probably the first method of popping corn was by tossing it into the fire or hot ashes – and catching it as it came right back at you. Today's method varies little. You can pop corn in a little oil in a covered frying pan or, if you are an addict, in an automatic, success-guaranteed popper. Success is virtually assured anyway, for growers of branded corn assert that 99 percent of it will pop, thanks to continuing research programs.

Popped corn is high in fiber, low in calories (it can be as low as 25 calories for one cup of corn) and a useful source of vitamins, minerals and protein. So far, so good! It's up to you whether you toss it in butterscotch dressing or peanut butter and ruin it all!

Since the development of contact grills and sandwich toasters, a new snacking fashion has developed - the toasted sandwich. Use wholemeal bread for maximum fiber and gather together your own choice of delicacies and left-overs for the fillings. Lean meat, poultry and fish, slices of vegetables and fresh fruits will keep the fat content to a minimum. With a bowl of soup and a fresh salad, a sizzling sandwich can make a meal as tasty, healthy and satisfying as any.

For spur-of-the-moment snacks to serve with drinks or salads, it pays to have some cottage or cream cheese on hand to whizz up with avocado, banana, anchovies, almonds or whatever.

Use these dips and spreads as toasted sandwich fillings, in hot pitta bread, in jumbo French bread slices, to fill celery boats, scooped-out cucumber, tomatoes and pears, stoned peaches and avocado halves. If you go to a "bring a dish" party, as so many Americans do, a dip is always a welcome addition to the table.

Eggs - fried sunny-side-up or easy-over (fried on both sides); baked with peppers and sausages; tossed with corned beef to make a melt-in-the-mouth hash; steamed over salt beef and beetroots in red flannel hash; stirred into Mexican rice – eggs are a snacker's protein-packed staple. Pan-fried pizzas, pancakes, jacket potatoes and canned tortillas for Tex-Mex enchiladas, all have endless possibilities for filling snacks with countless permutations. In this chapter we explore some of them.

HOMESTEAD EGGS

Photograph on page 144

Apples cooked with pork products have a long association in New England homes. This is a good breakfast dish.

50 g/2 oz butter
2 medium onions, sliced into
    rings
4 pork sausages, sliced
2 dessert apples, cored and
    sliced
6 eggs
salt and pepper

Serves 3

Melt the butter in a frying-pan and fry the onion and sausages over moderate heat, stirring frequently, for 5 minutes. Add the apples, stir well and break in the eggs. Cover the pan and cook for 3-5 minutes, until the eggs are cooked as you like them. Some Americans serve out the onions, sausages and apples, flip over the eggs and fry the second side for a minute or two – known as "easy over."

EGG AND BACON SKILLET

Quick and easy and straight from the fire, an old farmhouse recipe that's perfect for breakfast or brunch.

250 g/8 oz back or streaky
    bacon rashers
90 ml/6 tbls milk
15 ml/1 tbls flour
4 eggs
salt and pepper
a large pinch of nutmeg
25 g/1 oz butter
4 tomatoes, sliced
parsley sprigs, to garnish

Serves 2-3

Cut the rind from the bacon and broil for 2-3 minutes, until golden brown.

Gradually pour the milk onto the flour to make a smooth paste. Beat in the eggs one at a time and season with salt, pepper and nutmeg. Melt half of the butter in a small frying-pan, and swirl it to cover the base. When the butter is just turning brown, pour in the egg mixture and cook over moderately high heat, lifting the edges with a spatula occasionally, until it is set.

Arrange the bacon rashers and the tomatoes on top. Melt the remaining butter and brush onto the tomatoes. Broil for 2-3 minutes. Garnish with the parsley and serve at once.

ROUND-THE-CLOCK BAKED EGGS

From breakfast to late, late supper, here's a nourishing dish packed with color and texture.

45 ml/3 tbls vegetable oil
1 medium onion, chopped
4 medium potatoes, cooked
    and diced
2 green peppers, seeded and
    chopped
8 small sausages, sliced
250-g/8-oz can tomatoes
2.5 ml/½ tsp dried oregano
8 eggs
salt and pepper

Serves 4

Heat the oil in a flameproof dish and fry the onion over moderate heat for 3 minutes, stirring once or twice. Add the potatoes, peppers and sausage slices and cook for 10 minutes, stirring frequently. Add the tomatoes and oregano, stir well and cook for a further 10 minutes.

Break the eggs over the vegetables, season with salt and pepper and cover with foil. Bake in the oven at 180C/350F/gas 4 for 12-15 minutes until the eggs are lightly set. Serve at once, with triangles of toast.

RANCHER'S EGGS

2 large tomatoes, peeled and
    diced
1 medium onion, finely
    chopped
1 clove garlic, crushed
salt
5 ml/1 tsp chopped coriander
    leaves
100-g/4-oz can mild green
    chillies, diced
4 tortillas
vegetable oil, for frying
25 g/1 oz butter
1 medium onion, thinly sliced
    into rings
4 eggs
50 g/2 oz grated cheese

Serves 4

Simmer the tomatoes, chopped onion, garlic, salt, coriander and chillies in a covered pan over moderate heat for 10 minutes, stirring occasionally. Keep the sauce warm.

Fry the tortillas in oil for 1-2 minutes, to soften them. Drain them on kitchen paper.

Melt the butter and 15 ml/1 tbls oil and fry the onion rings until they are translucent. Remove them from the pan and fry the eggs.

Place the tortillas on a baking sheet and place a fried egg in the center of each. Spoon the chilli sauce around the eggs. Sprinkle with the onion rings and cheese. Cook under a moderately hot grill until the cheese melts.

RED FLANNEL HASH

Here's the traditional way to give salt beef a second showing. The addition of beetroot gives the dish its color and unusual name.

750 g/1½ lb cooked salt beef,
   finely minced
225 g/8 oz cooked beetroot,
   peeled and chopped
350 g/12 oz cooked and
   mashed potatoes
1 large onion, finely chopped
salt and pepper
50 g/2 oz butter
150 ml/¼ pt thick cream
8 eggs
a pinch of paprika

Serves 4

Stir the beetroot, potatoes and onion into the minced meat and beat the mixture well until it is smooth. Season with salt and pepper. Melt the butter in a heavy-based frying-pan and, when it is hot, spread the meat mixture evenly. Fry without stirring over moderately high heat for 15 minutes, until a brown crust forms on the underside.

   Pour the cream over the top and press 8 indentations in the top with the back of a large spoon. Break an egg into each and season with salt, pepper and paprika. Cover the pan and cook for a further 10-12 minutes over moderate heat until the eggs are lightly cooked. Serve at once, straight from the pan.

BREAKFAST PANCAKES

These pancakes make bacon and eggs into a hearty meal. Not only that, they are super with maple syrup, molasses syrup or honey.

125 g/4 oz self-raising flour
5 ml/1 tsp baking powder
2.5 ml/½ tsp salt
1 egg
30 ml/2 tbls vegetable oil
150 ml/¼ pt milk
oil or butter, for frying

Makes 12 pancakes

Sift together flour, baking powder and salt. Make a well in the center and beat in the egg and the oil. Gradually pour on the milk, beating constantly.

   Grease a frying-pan with a little oil or butter. When the pan is hot, drop 15 ml/1 tablespoons of the batter, well apart, and cook over moderately high heat until the pancakes bubble and are golden brown on the undersides. Flip over and brown on the other sides. Keep the pancakes warm while you cook the rest of the batter.

   (For sweet pancakes, sift 30 ml/2 tbls caster sugar and 2.5 ml/½ tsp ground cinnamon with the flour. For herb pancakes stir in 5 ml/1 tsp dried oregano or basil and season with pepper.)

CHICKEN ENCHILADAS

Most cooks agree that canned tortillas are perfect for snacks as making your own is something of a specialist occupation. This type of dish is served throughout the South-West and is typical of the Tex-Mex cuisine - authentic in origin, but greatly simplified.

12 canned tortillas
30 ml/2 tbls vegetable oil
4 rashers bacon, rind
   removed, chopped
2 medium onions, finely
   chopped
1 clove garlic, crushed
5-10 ml/1-2 tsp chilli powder,
   or to taste
15 ml/1 tbls flour
90 ml/6 tbls tomato purée
400-g/14-oz can tomatoes
a pinch of crushed cumin
   seeds
salt
500 g/1 lb cooked chicken,
   chopped
75 g/3 oz grated Parmesan
   cheese

Serves 4

Heat the oil and fry the bacon, onions and garlic over moderate heat for 4 minutes, stirring frequently. Stir in the chilli powder and flour, then the tomato purée, tomatoes and cumin. Season with salt, bring to the boil and simmer for 25-30 minutes, until the sauce is thick.

   Mix just enough of the sauce with the chicken to moisten it. Spoon the chicken mixture into the center of each tortilla, roll up and arrange in a baking dish, seam side down. Pour over the remaining sauce and sprinkle with the cheese.

   Bake in the oven at 180C/350F/gas 4 for 25 minutes. Serve hot.

SKEWERED BACON POTATOES

Jacket potatoes with soured cream, jacket potatoes with *anything*, are a favorite American snack. Here they are jauntily topped with bacon rolls.

4 large potatoes, scrubbed,
   dried and pricked
8 rashers streaky bacon
4 prunes, stoned
75 g/3 oz butter
2 large onions, cut into rings

Serves 4

Cook the potatoes in the oven at 200C/400F/gas 6 for about 1 hour, or until they are soft.

Cut the rind from the bacon, cut each rasher in half and stretch pieces with the back of a knife. Cut each prune lengthways into 4 strips. Wrap each piece of bacon around a prune strip and thread them onto 4 small skewers. Cook under a medium grill, turning once.

Melt half the butter in a frying-pan and fry the onion rings until they are golden brown.

Cut a cross in the top of each potato. Divide the remaining butter and the onion rings between them and top with the skewers. Serve at once, with Spiced tomato sauce (page 170).

DIPS AND SPREADS

Dips can hold their own on all kinds of occasions. Serve them as an appetizer with drinks, accompanied by crisp and crunchy straws of fresh vegetables and twig-like cocktail biscuits, or spread on savory biscuits or toast; with sausages, scoops of pitta bread or pumpernickel fingers for a teenage party; or with a choice of salads for a summer meal.

Avocado Cheese Dip

1 large, ripe avocado, halved, stoned and peeled
125 g/4 oz cottage cheese
20 ml/4 tsp lemon juice
1 small onion, quartered
salt and pepper
a few drops Worcestershire sauce

Makes 250 g/8 oz dip

Liquidize all the ingredients in a blender until smooth - or mash the avocado and beat it with the sieved cheese and lemon juice. Finely chop the onion and stir into the mixture. Season with salt, pepper and the sauce.

Liptauer Cheese Dip

50 g/2 oz unsalted butter, softened
125 g/4 oz full-fat cream cheese
5 ml/1 tsp made-mustard
10 ml/2 tsp capers, chopped
5 ml/1 tsp paprika pepper
5 ml/1 tsp anchovy paste
15 ml/1 tbls chopped chives

Makes 175 g/6 oz dip

Beat together all the ingredients (except the chives) until the mixture is smooth. Stir in 10 ml/2 tsp of the chives and garnish with the remainder.

Blue Cheese and Walnut Dip

125 g/4 oz unsalted butter, softened
125 g/4 oz full-fat cream cheese
60 ml/4 tbls single cream
125 g/4 oz Roquefort cheese, crumbled
50 g/2 oz chopped walnuts

Makes 450 g/14 oz dip

Beat together the butter and cream cheese, then beat in the cream. Stir in the blue cheese and walnuts.

Domino Dip

250 g/8 oz full-fat cream cheese
100-g/3½-oz jar black lumpfish roe
5 ml/1 tsp lemon juice

Makes 350 g/12 oz dip

Beat the cheese until it is soft, stir in the roe and lemon juice. If necessary, thin with a little cream or top of the milk.

Banana and Date Dip

250 g/8 oz cottage cheese, sieved
2 medium bananas, mashed
50 g/2 oz pitted dates, finely chopped
10 ml/2 tsp orange juice
thin slices of orange, to garnish

Makes 500 g/1 lb dip

Beat together the cheese and bananas. Stir in the dates and then the orange juice, a little at a time. Garnish with slices of orange.

Baked Bean Dip

This dip can be served hot, with sausage or pitta bread, dip-sticks, or cold with biscuits and crudités.

225-g/8-oz can baked beans
45 ml/3 tbls horseradish mustard
15 ml/1 tbls tomato ketchup
30 ml/2 tbls vinegar
1 small onion, chopped
salt and pepper

Makes 275 g/10 oz dip

Liquidize all the ingredients in a blender. Heat gently without boiling and season with salt and pepper.

Aubergine Dip

This is a variation of a salad popular in Greece and Turkey, at its best when served with hot pitta bread.

1 large aubergine
250 g/8 oz full-fat cream cheese
6 spring onions, white part only, finely chopped
salt and pepper

Makes about 500 g/1 lb dip

Prick the aubergine skin all over and broil under a hot grill, turning frequently, for 20 minutes, until the skin has turned black and the aubergine has collapsed.

Cool under cold water and remove the skin. Purée the flesh in a liquidizer. When it is cold, beat it with the cheese and stir in the onions. Season with salt and pepper.

Smoked Mackerel Dip

This is especially good with pumpernickel or rye, or on hot buttered toast.

125 g/4 oz unsalted butter,
  softened
125 g/4 oz full-fat cream
  cheese
45 ml/3 tbls soured cream
350 g/12 oz smoked mackerel
  fillets, skinned and flaked
30 ml/2 tbls lemon juice
15 ml/1 tbls chopped chives
salt and pepper

Makes 600 g/1¼ lb dip

Beat the butter and beat in the cheese and soured cream. Stir in the mackerel, lemon juice and chives and season with salt and pepper.

Almond Crunch Dip

4 rashers bacon, rind
  removed, finely chopped
250 g/8 oz full-fat cream
  cheese
30 ml/2 tbls mayonnaise
2 spring onions, finely
  chopped
10 ml/2 tsp chopped parsley
salt and pepper
150 g/5 oz blanched almond
  halves, toasted

Makes 500 g/1 lb dip

Fry the bacon in a non-stick pan until it is crisp and dry. Beat together the cheese and mayonnaise, stir in the bacon, onions and parsley and season with salt and pepper. Just before serving, stir in the almonds, reserving a few to garnish.

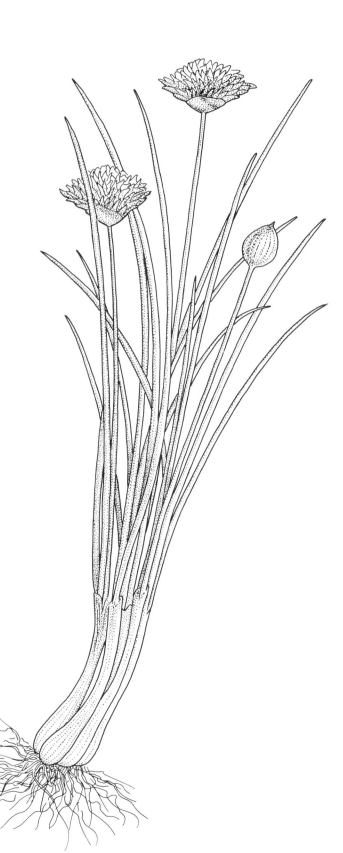

SALAMI OPEN SANDWICH

Photograph opposite

However simple the ingredients for open sandwiches, they
need to be presented in an appetizing way – like this.

1 slice rye crispbread
butter
1 thin slice cheese, such as
    Double Gloucester
2-3 small lettuce leaves
3 thin slices salami, skinned
25 g/1 oz cream cheese
1 stuffed olive, sliced
3 thin slices cucumber
parsley sprigs, to garnish

Serves 1

Butter the crispbread and cover it with the cheese slice and
lettuce leaves. Wrap the salami slices into cones and pipe
cream cheese to fill them. Arrange them on the lettuce and
garnish each one with a slice of olive. Cut each slice of
cucumber from the skin through to the center, twist into a
letter S and arrange between the salami. Garnish with the
parsley.
    Pumpernickel or black rye bread are good bases for open
sandwiches, too.

TOASTED SANDWICHES

The introduction of contact grills and sandwich toasters has brought a new element of fast foods into our kitchens, one with endless possibilities. Dress up the sandwiches with salad garnishes, fresh fruits, a selection of sauces and chutneys, and they make a "proper" meal.

Maryland Chicken Sandwiches

4 medium thick slices bread,
    crusts removed
softened butter, for spreading
125 g/4 oz cooked chicken,
    finely chopped
1 large banana, mashed
30 ml/2 tbls canned
    sweetcorn, drained
salt and pepper
5 ml/1 tsp mango sauce
    (optional)

Makes 2 sandwiches

Spread the bread on both sides with the butter and heat the appliance. Mix together the chicken, banana and sweetcorn, season with salt and pepper and stir in the mango sauce, if used. Spread the filling onto two slices of bread and cover with the others. Broil for 3-4 minutes, or according to the instructions for your appliance. Serve hot with salads and chutneys.

Chicken and Pineapple Sandwiches

4 medium thick slices bread,
    crusts removed
softened butter, for spreading
125 g/4 oz cooked chicken,
    finely chopped
45 ml/3 tbls canned pineapple
    pieces, drained
30 ml/2 tbls mango chutney,
    chopped

Makes 2 sandwiches

Spread the bread with the butter on both sides and heat the appliance. Mix together the chicken, pineapple and chutney and divide between two slices of bread. Cover with the other slice. Broil for 3-4 minutes, or as directed with your appliance.

Prawn Sandwiches

4 medium thick slices bread,
    crusts removed
50 g/2 oz unsalted butter,
    softened
2 cloves garlic, crushed
5 ml/1 tsp chopped parsley
5 ml/1 tsp lemon juice
1 hard-boiled egg, chopped
75 g/3 oz cooked shelled
    prawns, chopped
45 ml/3 tbls mayonnaise
a pinch of cayenne pepper

Makes 2 sandwiches

Beat the garlic and parsley into the butter and then, a few drops at a time, the lemon juice. Spread the bread on both sides with the garlic butter. Heat the appliance. Mix together the egg, prawns and mayonnaise and season with cayenne. Divide the filling between two slices of bread and cover with the others. Broil for 3-4 minutes, or as directed for your appliance.

Liver Pâté and Herb Sandwiches

4 medium thick slices bread,
    crusts removed
softened butter, for spreading
75 g/3 oz soft liver pâté
5 ml/1 tsp Dijon mustard
1 hard-boiled egg, chopped
10 ml/2 tsp chopped chervil
5 ml/1 tsp chopped chives
salt and pepper

Makes 2 sandwiches

Spread the bread with the butter on both sides and heat the appliance. Beat the pâté and beat in the mustard, egg and herbs and season with salt and pepper. Divide the filling between two slices of bread and cover with the others. Broil for 3-4 minutes, or as directed for your appliance.

Crab and Cream Cheese Sandwiches

4 medium thick slices bread,
    crusts removed
softened butter, for spreading
50 g/2 oz full-fat cream cheese
15 ml/1 tbls soured cream
50 g/2 oz dressed crab
salt and pepper
5 ml/1 tsp lemon juice

Makes 2 sandwiches

Spread the bread on both sides with the butter and heat the appliance. Beat together the cheese, soured cream and crab and season well with salt and pepper. Stir in the lemon juice. Divide the filling between two slices of bread and cover with the others. Broil for 3-4 minutes, or as directed for your appliance.

Apricot and Ginger Sandwiches

4 medium thick slices bread,
    crusts removed
softened butter, for spreading
50 g/2 oz cottage cheese
4 canned apricot halves,
    drained and chopped
1 piece preserved ginger,
    drained and finely chopped
30 ml/2 tbls demerara sugar
2.5 ml/½ tsp ground ginger

Makes 2 sandwiches

Spread the bread on both sides with the butter. Beat together the cheese, apricots and ginger and divide the filling between two slices of bread. Cover with the other two slices and broil for 3-4 minutes, or as directed for your appliance. Mix together the sugar and ginger, sprinkle over the sandwiches and serve at once.

Peanut and Apple Sandwiches

4 medium thick slices bread,
    crusts removed
softened butter, for spreading
45 ml/3 tbls crunchy peanut
    butter
1 large dessert apple, peeled,
    cored and grated or finely
    chopped
30 ml/2 tbls unsalted peanuts,
    roughly chopped

Makes 2 sandwiches

Spread the bread on one side with the butter. Mix together the peanut butter, apple and peanuts and spread on the unbuttered side of two slices. Complete the sandwiches, buttered sides out. Broil for 3-4 minutes or as directed for your appliance.

MICHIGAN TONGUE SANDWICH

4 crusty bread rolls
1 recipe baked bean dip (page
    150), cold
8 lettuce leaves, shredded
4 slices cooked tongue
1 small avocado, halved,
    stoned and sliced
60 ml/4 tbls mayonnaise
salt and pepper

Makes 4 rolls

Split the rolls and pull out the soft bread in the center. Spread one half of the rolls with baked bean dip, cover with half the shredded lettuce, then with the tongue, avocado slices and mayonnaise. Season with salt and pepper and top with the remaining lettuce.

DOUBLE DECKER SANDWICHES

Photograph on page 142

There's a great fancy for high-rise sandwiches with a bit-of-this and a bit-of-that from the refrigerator and store cupboard. It's the snacking equivalent of a one-pot meal.

3 slices rye bread
butter, for spreading
4 lettuce leaves
2 large tomatoes, thinly sliced
30 ml/2 tbls potato salad,
    chopped
25 g/1 oz smoked salmon,
    thinly sliced
8 thin slices cucumber
45 ml/3 tbls mayonnaise
pepper
50 g/2 oz hard country cheese,
    such as Leicester
2 large radishes, thinly sliced
3 chicory leaves
1 radish rose, to garnish
celery leaves, to garnish

Serves 1

Spread the bread slices with butter. On the bottom slices arrange two lettuce leaves, tomato, potato salad, smoked salmon, cucumber and mayonnaise and season with pepper.

  Cover the second slice and arrange lettuce leaves, cheese, radish, chicory, smoked salmon and cress. Top with mayonnaise and season with pepper.

  Cover with the third bread slice and garnish with a radish rose and celery leaf.

SALAMI AND CHEESE SANDWICHES

You can serve these salami wedges as cocktail snacks or as part of a salad meal.

250 g/8 oz salami, skinned
    and thinly sliced
250 g/8 oz full-fat cream
    cheese
2 dill cucumbers, finely
    chopped
1 clove garlic, crushed
pepper
24 stuffed green olives
lettuce leaves, to serve

Serves 8-12

Beat together the cream cheese, chopped cucumber and garlic and season with pepper. Spread the cheese mixture over the salami, building up stacks of 4 salami slices sandwiched together with cheese. Cut each stack into quarters, or eighths if they are to be served as cocktail snacks. Pierce each salami wedge with a cocktail stick spearing an olive. Serve them on a bed of lettuce.

BAKED TUNA TOASTIES

Photograph opposite (at center)

4 slices cut from a small white
 loaf
about 25 g/1 oz butter
225-g/7-oz can tuna fish,
 drained
10 ml/2 tsp mayonnaise
2 eggs, separated
15 ml/1 tbls chopped parsley
salt and pepper
75 g/3 oz grated cheese
parsley sprigs, to garnish

Serves 4

Cut the crusts from the bread and spread the slices with
butter. Mix together the tuna, mayonnaise, egg yolks and
parsley and season with salt and pepper. Spread the filling
evenly over the bread. Whisk the egg whites until stiff and
fold in the cheese. Spread over the tuna mixture.

Place the bread on a baking tray and bake at 200C/400F/gas 6
for 15 minutes, or until the cheese meringue is golden brown.
Garnish with the parsley and serve at once.

CHICKEN AND SWEETCORN BAPS

Photograph opposite (at bottom)

75 g/3 oz butter
1 large onion, sliced
45 ml/3 tbls flour
150 ml/¼ pt milk
150 ml/¼ pt chicken stock
 (page 12)
75 g/3 oz canned sweetcorn,
 drained
175 g/6 oz cooked chicken,
 chopped
15 ml/1 tbls Worcestershire
 sauce
salt and pepper
4 baps
2 large tomatoes, sliced
5 ml/1 tsp chopped chives, to
 garnish

Serves 4

Melt 50 g/2 oz of the butter and fry the onion over low heat for
5 minutes, until it is soft. Stir in the flour, then gradually pour
on the milk and stock, stirring. Bring the sauce to the boil and
simmer for 3 minutes. Stir in the sweetcorn, chicken and
Worcestershire sauce and season well with salt and pepper.

Cut the baps in half and toast them on both sides. Spread
them on one side with the remaining butter and divide the
filling between them. Garnish each bap with a tomato slice
sprinkled with chives. Serve hot.

PAN-FRIED PIZZA

400-g/14-oz can tomatoes
1 large onion, chopped
1 clove garlic, crushed
2.5 ml/½ tsp dried mixed
 herbs
2.5 ml/½ tsp dried oregano
salt and pepper
8 stuffed green olives,
 chopped
150 g/6 oz self-raising flour
2.5 ml/½ tsp baking powder
50 g/2 oz margarine
90-105 ml/6-7 tbls milk
250 g/8 oz grated cheese
2 green peppers, seeded and
 thinly sliced
40-g/1¾-oz can anchovy
 fillets, drained

Serves 4

Tip the can of tomatoes into a pan, stir in the onion, garlic and
herbs and season with salt and pepper. Bring to the boil and
cook for 10-12 minutes, until the sauce has thickened to a
spreadable consistency. Check the seasoning and stir in the
olives.

Sift the flour and baking powder and rub in the margarine
until the mixture resembles fine breadcrumbs. Pour in just
enough milk to form a soft dough. Turn the dough onto a
lightly-floured surface and knead until smooth. Shape into a
20-cm/8-in round.

Well-grease a 20-cm/8-in non-stick frying pan and slide the
dough round into it. Cover the pan with a lid or foil and cook
gently over low heat for about 15-20 minutes, or until the
dough is well risen. Spread the tomato mixture evenly over the
surface. Cover with the grated cheese, then make a lattice
pattern with the pepper strips and anchovies.

Cook the pizza under a moderately hot grill until the
topping is bubbling and brown. Serve at once.

SPEEDY PIZZAS

Photograph opposite (at top)

2 baps
125 g/4 oz grated cheese
60 ml/4 tbls tomato ketchup
60 ml/4 tbls tomato juice
10 ml/2 tsp German mustard
2.5 ml/½ tsp mixed dried
 herbs
salt and pepper
8 anchovy fillets, drained
12 black olives, stoned

Serves 2

Cut each bap in half lengthways. Mix together the cheese,
ketchup, tomato juice, mustard and herbs and season with salt
and pepper. Divide the mixture between each bap. Arrange 2
anchovies in a cross on top of each and an olive in each corner.
Cook under a hot grill until bubbling. Serve at once.

CORN CAKES

Pancakes made with corn meal and known in the South as
Hush Puppies. They are served in place of potatoes with
fritters, bacon and egg, ham and fried fish.

250 g/8 oz corn meal, or
   polenta
10 ml/2 tsp baking powder
5 ml/1 tsp salt
1 large onion, grated
200 ml/7 fl oz milk
2 eggs, well beaten
oil, for greasing

Makes about 12 corn cakes

Mix together the corn meal, baking powder, salt and onion
and gradually pour on the milk and eggs, beating all the time.
Beat well until the batter is smooth.
   Grease a heavy-based pan and when it is hot pour on 30
ml/2 tablespoons of the battter. Fry for 1 minute on each side,
until the corncakes are golden brown. Drain on kitchen paper
and keep the cakes warm while you cook the remaining batter.
Serve hot.

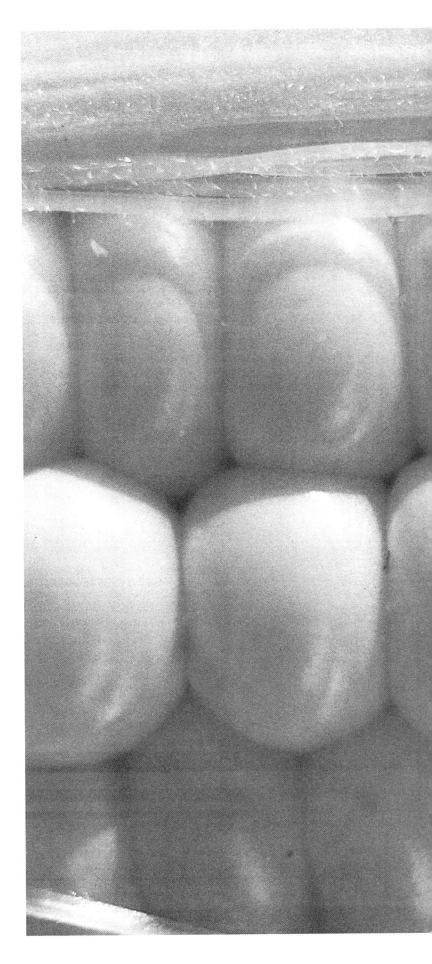

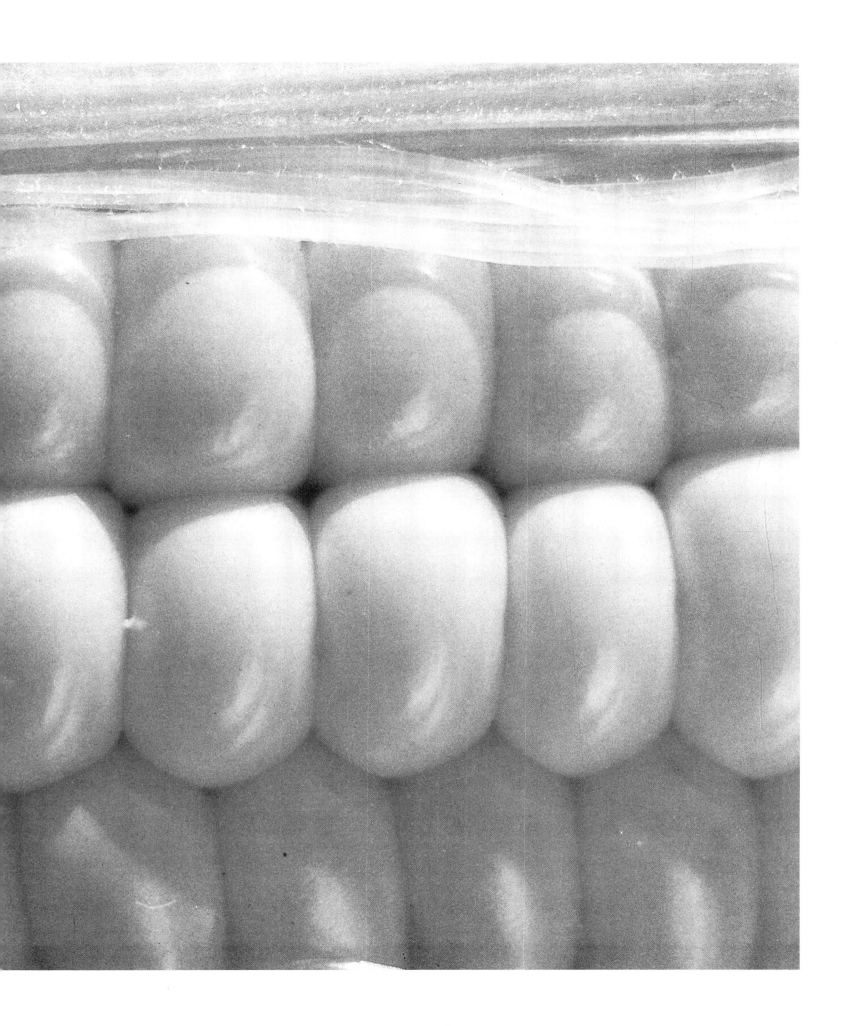

MEXICAN RICE

Photograph opposite

A cheap and cheerful dish to make on the spur of the moment.

15 ml/1 tbls vegetable oil
2 medium onions, thinly
 sliced
4 large pork sausages, thinly
 sliced
375 g/12 oz long-grain rice
750 ml/1¼ pt chicken stock
 (page 12), hot
8 small tomatoes, skinned and
 quartered
4 eggs
60 ml/4 tbls single cream
salt and pepper
a large pinch of cayenne
 pepper
15 ml/1 tbls chopped chives,
 to garnish

Serves 4

Heat the oil in a frying-pan and fry the onions over moderate heat for 2 minutes, stirring once or twice. Add the sausage slices, stir well, and cook for a further 2-3 minutes. Stir in the rice and pour on the stock. Bring to the boil, stir once, cover and simmer for 12 minutes. Add the tomatoes, stir, cover the pan and continue cooking for 3 minutes.

Beat the eggs and cream, season with salt, pepper and cayenne, pour over the rice and stir until the eggs are just set. Sprinkle with chives and serve at once.

POPCORN

Shaking pans or skillets of snap-crackle-and-popping corn is a fun way to snack. Imagination runs riot at the sweet and savory ways to glaze and flavor this protein-rich, fiber-full American cereal. Here are a few. Store popped corn in an airtight jar or tin.

Basic recipe

45 ml/3 tbls vegetable oil
45 ml/3 tbls popcorn kernels

This makes about 1 liter/¾ pt
   of popcorn

Pour the oil into a heavy frying-pan which has a lid. Add the kernels and shake them to coat with oil. Cover the pan and cook over high heat, shaking constantly, until the popping stops.
   Turn the popcorn into a dish and toss with melted butter, or any other flavoring you choose.

Cinnamon and Rosewater Popcorn

1 liter/1¾ pt popped popcorn
50 g/2 oz butter
50 g/2 oz caster sugar
5 ml/1 tsp ground cinnamon
15 ml/1 tbls rosewater

Melt the butter and sugar, stir in the cinnamon and rosewater. Toss the popcorn to coat it thoroughly.

Orange Popcorn

1 liter/1¾ pt popped popcorn
50 g/2 oz butter
50 g/2 oz soft light brown
   sugar
grated rind of 1 orange
15 ml/1 tbls orange flower
   water

Melt the butter and sugar and stir in the orange rind and orange flower water. Toss the popcorn to coat it thoroughly.

Honey Seed Popcorn

1 liter/1¾ pt popped popcorn
60 ml/4 tbls clear honey
60 ml/4 tbls peanut butter
60 ml/4 tbls dried milk
   powder
30 ml/2 tbls sesame seeds
30 ml/2 tbls sunflower seeds
60 ml/4 tbls desiccated
   coconut, toasted

Melt the honey and peanut butter and stir in the milk powder, seeds and coconut. Toss the popcorn to coat it thoroughly.

Dilly Corn

1 liter/1¾ pt popped popcorn
50 g/2 oz butter
grated rind of 1 lemon
15 ml/1 tbls dill seeds, lightly
   crushed
5 ml/1 tsp dried dill weed
salt and pepper

Melt the butter, stir in the lemon rind and herbs and season with salt and pepper. Toss the popcorn in the dressing to coat it thoroughly.

Mushroom and Bacon Popcorn

1 liter/1¾ pt popped popcorn
3 rashers bacon, rind
   removed, finely chopped
40 g/1½ oz butter
50 g/2 oz mushrooms, finely
   chopped
salt and pepper
5 ml/1 tsp Worcestershire
   sauce

Fry the bacon in a non-stick pan until it is crisp. Melt the butter and fry the mushrooms, stirring once or twice, for 2 minutes. Stir in the bacon and season with salt and pepper and the sauce. Toss the popcorn in the dressing to coat it thoroughly.

Butterscotch Corn

1 liter/1¾ pt popped popcorn
75 g/3 oz butter
100 ml/3½ fl oz molasses
75 g/3 oz soft light brown
   sugar
15 ml/1 tbls lemon juice
2.5 ml/½ tsp vanilla essence

Heat all the coating ingredients together, stirring frequently, to 141C/280F, the soft crack stage. Pour over the popcorn and toss to coat it thoroughly.
   This sticky butterscotch coating is perfect for making a popcorn mold. Pour it into a well-greased cake tin and shape it evenly over the base and around the sides. Leave it in the refrigerator for 30 minutes to set. Fill the mold with ice cream, fruit mousse or chiffon pie filling.

Pizza Popcorn

1 liter/1¾ pt popped popcorn
30 ml/2 tbls vegetable oil
1 small onion, finely chopped
1 clove garlic, crushed
45 ml/3 tbls tomato purée
15 ml/1 tbls dried oregano
50 g/2 oz grated Parmesan
   cheese

Heat the oil and fry the onion and garlic over moderate heat for 3 minutes, stirring frequently. Stir in the tomato purée and oregano with 30 ml/2 tbls water, season with salt and pepper, bring to the boil and simmer for 2 minutes. Toss the popcorn in the dressing to coat it thoroughly, then toss it in the cheese.

NO 2 WAGON

One of the early popcorn machines was this Cretors Number 2 Wagon.

9: PRESERVES

As we shake tomato sauce onto a sizzling barbecued chicken, contrast crisp and pungent vegetable pickle with a selection of smoked meats, or watch plum jelly melt into toasted muffins, it is hard to realize that these and other preserves originated from necessity. First and foremost, making store-cupboard preserves – sauce, relish, pickle, chutney, jam, jelly, mincemeat and fruit butter - was a practical means of preserving the fruits of one harvest until the next one came around – a whole year later. Fortunately, these preserves also added sweetness, piquancy, color and contrast to other preserved foods such as pickled and salted meat and fish, smoked ham and bacon, wind-dried sausages and, of course, to everyday things like bread and muffins.

Now that technology has provided other ways of storing foods safely – by drying, freezing, canning and vacuum packaging – and horticultural crops of all kinds can be staggered to give an extended period of harvest, these handy preserves are no longer a necessity. It is a mini-miracle that they have survived the food technological revolution at all.

In the early Colonial days, making preserves from locally-grown produce was of such importance that it became a joint venture. In the Pennsylvanian Dutch community, for example, spiced apple butter was made in huge vats outside the houses, each family taking turns to press the fruit and grind the spices.

The same German settlers (for "Dutch" is a corruption of "Deutsch") introduced pungent vegetable pickles into the American culinary repertoire – our recipe for Chow-chow constituted one of their traditional "sours."

Making preserves, one of the most therapeutic aspects of cooking, can nowadays still be a community venture, one family making a batch of applejack mincemeat and swapping half-a-dozen jars for a neighbor's pecan chutney.

There are just a few basic guidelines to ensure making successful preserves. Choose top quality fruit and vegetables that are very slightly under-ripe. Windfallen orchard fruits such as apples and pears may be used, when damaged parts can be cut away, but never include bruised produce of any kind. The persistent bacteria will eventually get the better of you!

Use stainless steel, enamel or aluminium pans, or ones with a non-stick finish. Where fruit and vegetables are left to stand overnight, layered with salt or sugar perhaps, always transfer them to a glass or pottery bowl.

For jam, jelly, fruit butters and mincemeat, transparent jam pot covers are adequate, but screw-on lids even better. And for all preserves with a high acid content, all pickles and chutneys, use lids with a non-corrosive lining. Coffee jars with plastic-lined lids are ideal.

Preserves were intended to be stored for a year and will cheerfully do so, given the right conditions. When the jars are cooled, label them clearly with the contents and date and store them in a cool, dry, airy place.

HUNGRY FAMILY JAM

When soft fruit was scarce in the homesteads it was eked out with the more plentiful late season's rhubarb. Hungry families didn't complain!

2 kg/4½ lb rhubarb, trimmed
　　and cut into 2.5-cm/1-in
　　pieces
150 ml/¼ pt unsweetened
　　orange juice, or water
3 kg/6½ lb sugar
1 kg/2¼ lb raspberries, hulled

Makes about 4.5 kg/10 lb

Put the rhubarb into a pan with the orange juice or water and simmer 10-15 minutes, or until the rhubarb is soft. Spread the sugar on baking trays and warm it in the oven at the lowest setting. Add the raspberries to the pan, bring to the boil and simmer for 15 minutes. Tip in the warmed sugar and stir over low heat until it has dissolved. Increase the heat, bring to the boil and fast-boil, stirring often, for 10-15 minutes, or until setting point is reached.

　　To test for set, remove the pan from the heat, put a little of the jam on a cold saucer and leave to cool. Push a finger across the surface. If it wrinkles, the jam is ready to pot. If not, boil for a further few minutes and test again.

　　Pour into hot, sterilized jars and cover with jam pot covers.

RED TOMATO JAM

Tomatoes are a low pectin fruit, but make a delicious jam when combined with the flavor and acidity of lemons.

2.75 kg/6 lb red tomatoes,
　　skinned and chopped
grated rind and juice of 6
　　lemons
2.75 kg/6 lb sugar
5 ml/1 tsp salt
10 ml/2 tsp ground ginger
2.5 ml/½ tsp ground allspice
2.5 ml/½ tsp ground
　　coriander

Makes about 3.5 kg/8 lb

Cook the tomatoes, lemon rind and juice in a pan until the mixture is thick and pulpy. Spread the sugar on baking trays and warm it in the oven at the lowest setting.

　　Tip the sugar into the pan, add the spices and stir over low heat until the sugar has dissolved. Increase the heat, bring to the boil and fast-boil, stirring often, for 15 minutes, or until setting point is reached (see previous recipe).

　　Pour the jam into hot, sterilized jars and cover with jam pot covers.

NEW ENGLAND PRESERVED QUINCES

This is a very rich preserve which is served chilled, as a dessert, with a bowl of thick cream. You can substitute apples or pears for up to one half of the quinces.

2.5 kg/5½ lb quinces
30 ml/2 tbls lemon juice
1.5 kg/3½ lb sugar

Makes about 1.5 kg/3½ lb

Scrub the quinces and remove stalks. Put the lemon juice in a bowl with about 1.5 liters/2¾ pt water. Peel, core and slice the quinces and drop the fruit straight into the acidulated water, to preserve the color. Put the quince cores and peel in a pan, add 750 ml/1½ pt water, bring to the boil and boil for 15 minutes. Strain the liquid and discard the peelings; strain the quince slices and add them to this liquid. Bring slowly to the boil and simmer for 30 minutes, or until the quince slices are tender. Remove the quince slices with a draining spoon and set aside.

　　Add the sugar to the liquid in the pan and stir over low heat until it has dissolved. Bring to the boil, add the quince slices and boil until the preserve clears and is transparent. Pour into hot, sterilized jars and cover with plastic-lined screw-on lids.

SPICED CRABAPPLES

Crabapples growing wild in New England, and too bitter for dessert, were made into delicious preserves.

2 kg/4½ lb crabapples
2 lemons
2 sticks cinnamon
5 ml/1 tsp whole cloves
1 piece root ginger, crushed
1 liter/1¾ pt dry cider
2 kg/4½ lb sugar

Makes about 2.5 kg/5½ lb

Pick the stalks from the crabapples. Thinly pare the rind from the lemons and squeeze out the juice. Tie the lemon rind, cinnamon, cloves and ginger into a piece of muslin. Put the lemon juice, cider and sugar into a pan with the bag of spices and 600 ml/1 pt water and stir over low heat until the sugar has dissolved. Bring to the boil and boil for 5 minutes.

　　Add the whole crabapples, return to the boil and simmer for 7-8 minutes, until the apples are just tender but not collapsing. Transfer the apples to a bowl and boil the syrup for a further 3 minutes. Pour it over the apples, cover and leave for 24 hours.

　　Return the fruit, syrup and spices to the pan, bring to the boil and boil for 3 minutes, stirring once or twice. Discard the spices. Spoon the fruit into hot, sterilized preserving jars and pour on the syrup to cover the fruit. Cover the jars with non-corrosive lids, stand them in a deep pan on a trivet or wad of papers so that they do not touch, and fill the pan with hot water. Simmer for 20 minutes. Remove the jars from the pan, tightly close the lids and leave to cool.

APPLEJACK MINCEMEAT

In Colonial days mincemeat was made with minced venison or beef, but now meat is rarely included. This preserve is delicious in tarts or flans, especially topped with sliced apples or pears and soured cream.

1 kg/2¼ lb green tomatoes,
    finely chopped
1 kg/2¼ lb cooking apples,
    peeled, cored and cubed
350 g/12 oz shredded suet
500 g/1 lb currants
500 g/1 lb seedless raisins
500 g/1 lb sultanas
500 g/1 lb chopped mixed
    candied peel
750 g/1½ lb soft dark brown
    sugar
10 ml/2 tsp salt
5 ml/1 tsp grated nutmeg
5 ml/1 tsp ground allspice
5 ml/1 tsp ground cinnamon
2.5 ml/½ tsp ground cloves
300 ml/½ pt applejack,
    Calvados or cider

Makes about 4 kg/9 lb

Put all the ingredients, except the last, into a pan, stir over very low heat until the juices run and the sugar has dissolved. Simmer very gently for 2½-3 hours, adding a very little water if needed.
    Remove from the heat and stir in the applejack or other liquor. Pack into warmed, sterilized jars, cover with waxed paper discs and plastic-lined screw-on lids. Alternatively, cool the preserve, pack in rigid containers, seal and freeze.

PUMPKIN CREAM

Made with pumpkin and other squashes, this is a short-keeping preserve with the texture of lemon curd. It is delicious at tea-time with hot muffins.

2-kg/4½-lb pumpkin,
    skinned, seeded and diced
5 ml/1 tsp ground allspice
2 kg/4½ lb sugar
250 g/8 oz unsalted butter
grated rind and juice of 4
    lemons
grated rind and juice of 1
    orange

Makes about 2.75 kg/6¼ lb

Steam the pumpkin in a colander over rapidly boiling water, or simmer it in a very little water for 15-20 minutes, or until it is tender. Strain the pumpkin (if simmered) and liquidize it in a blender or press through a sieve.
    Put the purée in a pan with the allspice, sugar, butter, lemon and orange rind and juice and stir over low heat until the sugar has dissolved. Bring to the boil and boil for 5 minutes, stirring occasionally. Beat well, then cool slightly.
    Pour the "cream" into hot, clean jars, cover with jam pot covers or plastic-lined screw-on lids and leave to cool. Store in the refrigerator.
    A mixture of granulated and soft light brown sugar makes a deliciously rich preserve.

PLUM JELLY

Use firm, slightly under-ripe plums (or damsons) to make this deep rose-colored preserve. It's good to serve with poultry and game, to add a bitter sweetness to casseroles and sauces, and to glaze fruit flans.

1.5 kg/3½ lb plums
a strip of thinly pared orange
    rind
sugar (see method)

Makes about 1 kg/2¼ lb

Put the plums and orange rind in a pan with 600 ml/1 pt water and cook gently for about 1 hour, or until they are soft.
    Hang a jelly bag over a bowl (scald cloth bags in boiling water) and tip in the plums and juice. Leave undisturbed to strain for about 1 hour. Do not squeeze the bag, or the jelly will be cloudy.
    Measure the strained juice and return to the pan with 500 g/1 lb sugar to each 600 ml/1 pt juice. Increase the heat, bring to the boil and fast-boil for 15 minutes, stirring often, or until setting point is reached (see recipe for Hungry Family jam, facing page).
    Pour the jelly into hot, sterilized jars and cover with jam pot covers.

DUTCH APPLE BUTTER

This preserve was made at apple-harvest time in huge wooden vats outside the houses in the Pennsylvania Dutch community. Serve it as a spread on toast, muffins and buns or as a filling for tarts and flans.

1.5 kg/3½ lb cooking apples,
    chopped
750 ml/1¼ pt dry cider
375 g/12 oz soft light brown
    sugar
2.5 ml/½ tsp ground
    cinnamon
1.5 ml/¼ tsp ground cloves
1.5 ml/¼ tsp grated nutmeg

Makes about 1 kg/2¼ lb

Cook the apples and cider for about 20 minutes until the fruit is soft. Rub through a nylon sieve or purée in a mouli-legumes. Return the purée to the pan and add the sugar and spices. Stir over low heat until the sugar has dissolved, then bring slowly to the boil. Simmer very gently for 1 hour, stirring often, until the fruit butter is thick and smooth. There should be no pools of excess liquid.
    Pour into warm, sterilized jars, cover with waxed paper discs and then with paper covers or screw-on lids. Store for up to 3 months.
    For a long-keeping preserve, sterilize the jars of butter. Lightly screw on the lids, stand the jars in a deep pan on a trivet or wad of papers so that they are not touching, and fill the pan with hot water. Simmer for 20 minutes. Remove the jars from the pan, tightly close the lids and leave to cool.

LOVE APPLE CHUTNEY

Photograph on page 164

Tomatoes were first considered decorative but poisonous, and were later claimed to have aphrodisiacal qualities - hence the nickname "love apples." In 1893 Justices in the US Court pronounced them not a fruit, but a vegetable.

2.5 kg/6 lb ripe tomatoes,
   skinned and quartered
250 g/8 oz onions, thinly
   sliced
15 ml/1 tbls allspice berries
5-cm/2-in piece dried root
   ginger, peeled and crushed
2 dried red chillies, halved
15 ml/1 tbls salt
300 ml/½ pt malt vinegar
375 g/12 oz light Muscovado
   sugar

Makes about 1.75 kg/3¾ lb

Put the tomatoes and onions into a large pan. Tie the allspice, ginger and chillies in a piece of muslin and add them, together with the salt. Cook over low-moderate heat, stirring occasionally until the mixture is pulpy. Add the vinegar and sugar and stir over low heat until the sugar has dissolved. Simmer for 1 hour, or until the preserve thickens. Remove the spices.
   Pour into warmed jars, cover with waxed paper discs and vinegar-proof lids. Cool, label, and store for 4 weeks before using.

RHUBARB AND RAISIN CHUTNEY

Photograph on page 164

250 g/8 oz light Muscovado
   sugar
300 ml/½ pt cider vinegar
2.5 ml/½ tsp ground allspice
2.5 ml/½ tsp ground cloves
5 ml/1 tsp mustard seed
1.5 ml/¼ tsp celery seed
5 ml/1 tsp salt
2 large onions, chopped
500 g/1 lb rhubarb, thinly
   sliced
250 g/8 oz raisins

Makes about 750 g/1½ lb

Put the sugar, vinegar, spices and salt into a large pan with 150 ml/¼ pt water. Stir over low heat to dissolve the sugar. Bring to the boil and boil for 5 minutes. Add the onions and rhubarb, stir well, cover and simmer for 45 minutes.
   Add the raisins and simmer, uncovered, until the mixture is thick.
   Pour into warm jars, cover with waxed paper discs and vinegar-proof lids. Cool, label and store.

PENNSYLVANIA DUTCH CHOW-CHOW

Serve this colorful blend of fresh vegetables with cold meats or as part of a winter salad. It is a traditional preserve from the German (Deutsch) community in Pennsylvania.

4 small cucumbers, diced
2 red and 2 green peppers,
   seeded and cut into
   matchstick strips
1 small cauliflower, cut into
   florets
2 small, tender celery hearts
   (use the outer leaves for
   soup)
500 g/1 lb French beans,
   topped, tailed and cut into
   5-cm/2-in lengths
500 g/1 lb shallots or small
   button onions
500 g/1 lb green tomatoes
75 ml/5 tbls salt
1 liter/1¾ pt cider vinegar
500 g/1 lb soft light brown
   sugar
30 ml/2 tbls mustard seed
30 ml/2 tbls celery seed
30 ml/2 tbls ground turmeric
15 ml/1 tbls mustard powder
10 ml/2 tsp pepper

Makes about 3 kg/6½ lb

Mix together all the vegetables, sprinkle with the salt and cover with boiling water. Set aside for 2 hours.
   Put all the remaining ingredients in a large pan, stir over low heat until the sugar has dissolved, and bring to the boil.
   Rinse the vegetables under cold, running water, drain well and add to the spiced vinegar. Boil again and simmer, stirring often, for 20 minutes, or until the vegetables are just tender.
   Spoon the vegetables into hot, sterilized jars and pour on spiced vinegar to cover them. Cover the jars with plastic-lined screw-on lids.

SPICED TOMATO SAUCE

You need something tasty to shake on all those hamburgers -
and nothing can beat your own home-made sauce.

2.5 kg/5½ lb ripe tomatoes,
　roughly chopped
500 g/1 lb sugar
20 ml/4 tsp salt
1.5 ml/¼ tsp cayenne
5 ml/1 tsp paprika
2.5 ml/½ tsp grated nutmeg
2.5 ml/½ tsp ground ginger
300 ml/½ pt white distilled
　vinegar

Makes about 1.5 liters/2¾
　pints

Gently cook the tomatoes until they are soft, stirring
occasionally. In another pan, stir the sugar, salt, spices and
vinegar over low heat until the sugar has dissolved.

Rub the tomatoes through a nylon sieve or purée them in a
mouli-legumes, and stir them into the spiced vinegar. Bring to
the boil and boil gently for 20-25 minutes, or until the mixture
has thickened and a spoon leaves a trail in the pan.

Pour the sauce into hot, sterilized bottles, to within 2 cm/
¾ in of the top. Stand the bottles on a trivet or wad of paper in
a deep pan so that they do not touch each other.

Loosely screw on plastic-lined or other vinegar-proof tops.
Fill the pan with very hot water, bring to simmering point and
simmer for 30 minutes. Remove the bottles from the pan and
tighten the screw tops.

CHILLI SAUCE

A Tex-Mex quickie sauce that is ideal with burgers, grills and
barbecues. It stores in the refrigerator for up to 1 week, so
make it in advance for a patio party.

15 g/½ oz lard or dripping
1 medium onion, chopped
30 ml/2 tbls flour
600 g/1¼ lb canned tomatoes,
　chopped
50 g/2 oz canned green
　chillies, drained and finely
　chopped
2 cloves garlic, chopped
2.5 ml/½ tsp freshly ground
　black pepper
5 ml/1 tsp salt
30 ml/2 tbls red wine vinegar

Makes about 500 ml/18 fl oz

Melt the lard or dripping and fry the onion over moderate heat
for 5 minutes, stirring occasionally. Stir in the flour to make a
thick paste. Add the remaining ingredients, stir well and
bring to the boil. Simmer for 30 minutes, stirring occasionally,
until the sauce is thick.

Pour into hot, sterilized jars and cover with plastic-lined
screw-on lids.

MAINE CAULIFLOWER AND TOMATO PICKLE

A golden brown pickle spiced with mustard, peppercorns and
chillies to serve with cheese, cold meats or smoked sausage.

2 medium cauliflowers, cut
　into florets
2 large onions, sliced
1 medium cucumber,
　chopped
250 g/8 oz white cabbage,
　coarsely shredded
500 g/1 lb firm tomatoes,
　peeled and quartered
coarse salt
750 ml/1¼ pt white distilled
　vinegar
5 ml/1 tsp ground ginger
5 ml/1 tsp mustard powder
5 ml/1 tsp black peppercorns
2 dried red chillies, halved
　lengthways
250 g/8 oz soft dark brown
　sugar

Makes about 2.75 kg/6 lb

Layer the vegetables in a bowl and sprinkle each layer with
salt. Cover and leave for 24 hours. Rinse the vegetables under a
cold tap and drain well.

Put the vinegar, spices and sugar into a large pan, stir over
low heat until the sugar has dissolved, then bring to the boil.
Boil for 5 minutes. Add the vegetables, bring slowly to the boil
and simmer for 20 minutes.

Spoon the pickle into hot, sterilized jars and pour on
enough spiced vinegar to cover. Cover the jars with plastic-
lined screw-on lids.

WATERMELON RIND PICKLE

Nothing need be wasted. Once you've enjoyed the ice-cold sunset-colored fruit, there's this candied pickle to look forward to. You can chop it and use it, as you do citrus peel, in cakes, buns and scones.

1 large watermelon
1.5 kg/3½ lb sugar
500 ml/18 fl oz white distilled
    vinegar
4 drops oil of cloves
1 cinnamon stick
10 pieces preserved ginger,
    drained and chopped

Makes about 3 kg/6½ lb

Quarter the watermelon and discard the seeds. Cut off the rind with a 2.5-cm/1-in layer of flesh and chop it into cubes. Put the sugar, vinegar, oil of cloves and cinnamon stick in a pan, stir over low heat until the sugar has dissolved, then bring to the boil. Pour the syrup over the watermelon rind, cover and leave for about 12 hours.

Lift out the rind with a draining spoon, bring the syrup to the boil again, pour over the pickle and leave for 12 hours. Repeat once more. Discard the cinnamon.

Pack the rind into hot, sterilized preserving jars, dividing the chopped ginger between them. Reboil the syrup and pour it to cover the rind. Loosely screw on vinegar-proof lids. Stand the jars on a trivet or wad of paper in a deep pan so that they do not touch and fill the pan with hot water. Simmer for 20 minutes, remove the jars from the pan and tightly screw on the lids.

CORN RELISH

The relish tray is a feature of many New England restaurants, offering a selection of relishes to be eaten with a mound of cottage cheese and chives.

6 large fresh or frozen corn
    cobs, or 500 g/1 lb corn
    kernels
2 large red peppers, seeded
    and finely chopped
1 medium onion, finely
    chopped
175 g/6 oz white cabbage,
    finely shredded
10 ml/2 tsp mustard powder
15 ml/1 tbls salt
5 ml/1 tsp sugar
150 ml/¼ pt white distilled
    vinegar

Makes about 2 liters/3½ pints

Cut the kernels from the corncobs. Mix the kernels with the peppers, onions and cabbage. Mix the mustard powder, salt and sugar to a smooth paste with the vinegar and stir in 100 ml/3½ fl oz water. Pour the spiced vinegar over the vegetables. Bring to the boil and simmer over moderate heat for 45 minutes, stirring frequently, until the mixture has thickened. Taste and adjust seasoning if necessary.

Pour into hot, sterilized jars and cover with plastic-lined screw-on lids.

APPLE AND MOLASSES CHUTNEY

Photograph on page 164

Use moist, dark brown unrefined molasses sugar for a rich, deep flavor; this chutney is perfect with cheese.

2 kg/4½ lb cooking apples,
    peeled, cored and chopped
600 ml/1 pt cider vinegar
2 cloves garlic, crushed
750 g/1½ lb molasses sugar
250 g/8 oz seedless raisins
10 ml/2 tsp ground ginger
2.5 ml/½ tsp mixed ground
    spice
5 ml/1 tsp salt
a pinch of cayenne pepper

Makes about 1.5 kg/3½ lb

Put the apples in a pan with half the vinegar and the garlic and cook for 20-25 minutes until the fruit has collapsed.

Add the remaining vinegar, the sugar, raisins and spices and stir over low heat until the sugar has dissolved. Bring to the boil and simmer for 25-30 minutes, until the chutney is thick and all the moisture has evaporated.

Pour into hot, sterilized jars, cover with waxed paper discs and then with plastic-lined screw-on lids.

PECAN CHUTNEY

A moist, crunchy chutney to serve with cheese, cold meats or burgers. You can use walnuts instead.

1 kg/2¼ lb cooking apples,
    peeled, cored and chopped
125 g/4 oz shelled pecans,
    chopped
250 g/8 oz sultanas
grated rind and juice of 1
    orange
grated rind and juice of 1
    lemon
2.5 ml/½ tsp ground cloves
2.5 ml/½ tsp ground
    cinnamon
a pinch of grated nutmeg
5 ml/1 tsp salt
500 g/1 lb soft dark brown
    sugar
400 ml/14 fl oz cider vinegar

Makes about 1.5 kg/3½ lb

Put all the ingredients into a heavy pan and stir over low heat until the sugar has dissolved. Bring to the boil and simmer gently, stirring occasionally, for 1 hour, or until the preserve is thick.

Pour into warmed jars and cover with plastic-lined screw-on lids.

INDEX

Recipes are listed alphabetically within sections which broadly correspond to the chapter headings.

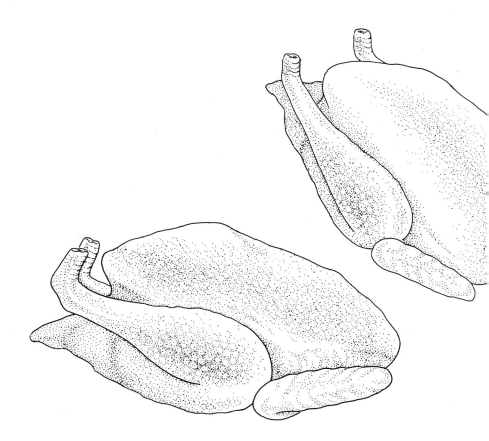

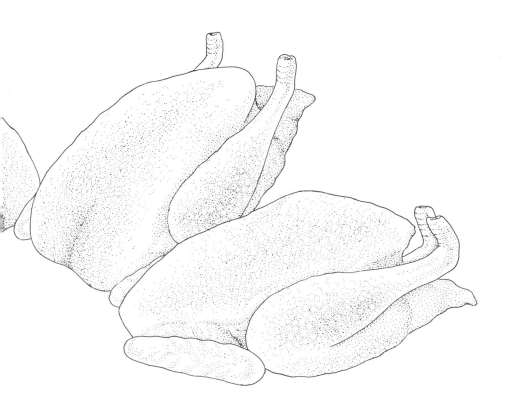

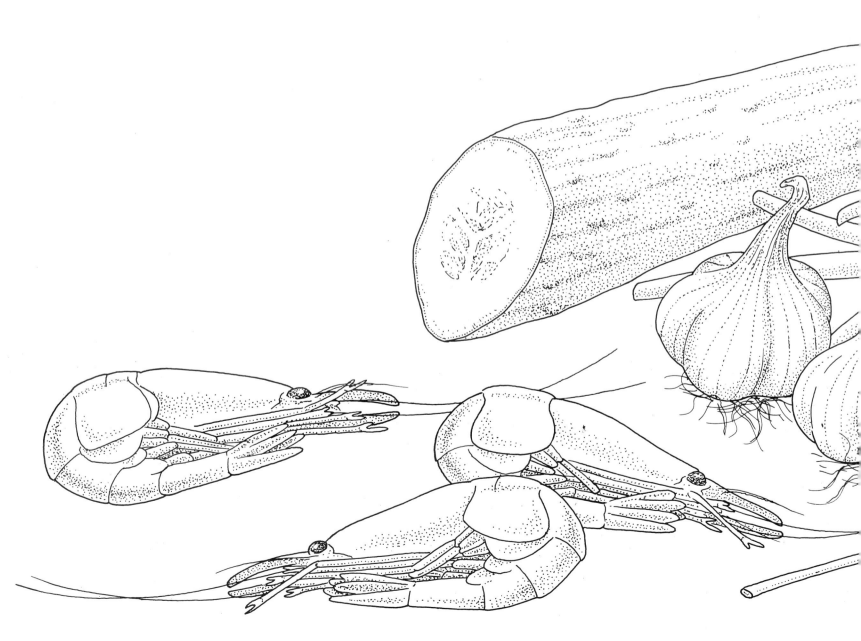

ACKNOWLEDGEMENTS

The Publishers wish to acknowledge their thanks to the following organisations for their help in the preparation of the colour photographs.

Allinsons:
Batch of bread
American Long-Grain Rice:
Meat loaf, Mexican rice, Southern-style picnic, Thanskgiving Dinner
Billingtons Sugar:
Creole Christmas Cake, Sultana squares, Spiced apple squares, Lemon fans, Peanut cookies, Love apple chutney, Rhubarb and raisin chutney, Apple and Molasses chutney
British Bacon Bureau:
Cauliflower and bacon salad
British Meat Promotition Executive:
Beef pot roast, Spiced lamb meatballs, Stir-fried beef and cauliflower, Beef goulash, Liver crumble
Colmans Mustard:
Boston baked beans, Chicken and ham burgers, Mustard soup, Courgette and walnut teabread, Savory griddle scones, Mustard scones, Kedgeree
Danish Agricultural Producers:
Skewered bacon potatoes, Raspberry and orange meringue, Bacon hotpot
Eggs Information Bureau:
Coffee bavarois, Waffles, Baked Alaska, Homestead eggs, Supper plait, Fruit sorbets
English Country Cheeses:
Double-decker sandwich
Flour Advisory Bureau:
Speedy pizzas, Chicken and sweetcorn baps, Baked tuna toasties
The Honey Bureau:
Marinated fish kebabs, Honey and mango mousse, Californian fruit salad, Pear beehives
Kelloggs:
Prawn and pepper flan, Christmas chocolate boxes
Mushroom Growers' Association:
Nut and mushroom pilaff, Deep-fried mushrooms
National Dairy Council:
Salami open sandwich, Dairy scones, Kiwi fruit surprise, Lobster pot ring
Pasta Information Centre:
Chicken scallops, Chicken lasagne, Vegetarian pasta salad, Spaghetti with clam sauce
St. Lucia Promotion:
St. Lucia pumpkin soup
Scottish Salmon Information Service:
Poached salmon
Sea Fish Industry Authority:
Southern crab soup, Fish and ham rolls, Cod Catalan
The Summer Orange Office:
Citrus cocktail

BY THE SAME AUTHOR

The High-Fibre Cookbook, Martin Dunitz
The 60-Minute Cookbook, Faber
One-pot Cooking, Fontana
The Everyday Gourmet, Granada
Bean Feast, Granada
Food for Keeps, Granada
The Complete Grill Cookbook, Granada
High-Fibre Vegetarian Cookery, Granada
Encyclopedia of Spices, Marshall Cavendish
The Hostess Cookbook, with Anne Ager, Octopus
A Taste of the Country, Penguin
The Busy Cook's Book, St. Michael